wired by God>>

wired by God>>

>> empowering your teen for a life of passion and purpose

joe white with larry weeden

Tyndale House Publishers, Inc.
Wheaton, Illinois

A Focus on the Family book published by
Tyndale House Publishers, Wheaton, Illinois 60189

TYNDALE is a registered trademark of Tyndale House Publishers, Inc. Tyndale's quill logo is a
trademark of Tyndale House Publishers, Inc.

All Scripture quotations, unless otherwise indicated, are taken from the *Holy Bible, New
International Version®*. NIV®. Copyright © 1973, 1978, 1984 by International Bible Society.
Used by permission of Zondervan Publishing House. All rights reserved.
Scripture quotations marked (KJV) are taken from the *King James Version*.

Some names and details of certain case studies in this book have been changed to protect the
privacy of the individuals involved. The events and underlying principles, however, have been
conveyed as accurately as possible.

Cover design: Brian Merculief
Cartoons: John Duckworth

ISBN 1-58997-162-0

Printed in the United States of America

table of contents

Part Four: Where Do You Go from Here?

how to use the CD-ROM

No doubt about it: This book will help you encourage your teen to discover how God has "wired" him or her. But you don't have to do all the work yourself. We've provided a tool your teen can use, too, on the CD-ROM that accompanies this book.

It's a guide for your teen's journey of self-discovery, a creative way to dream big dreams about the future. We don't want to call it a workbook, because it's too much fun. Your teen can read it onscreen; to make it interactive, just print it out a chapter at a time so that he or she can complete the exercises on paper. For best results, talk about what your teen is learning. The CD-ROM encourages that, too.

The CD-ROM includes the *Wired by God* teen guide in PDF (Portable Document Format). You'll need Adobe Acrobat Reader (already installed on many computers) to read the PDF file; if you don't have it, you can install it from the disk.

Here are a few technical things you'll want to know.

Since the PDF file is large, we recommend copying it to your hard drive and opening that copy—especially if you plan to print it out. Because printing large files can be slow, it's best to print out single chapters as you need them rather than producing the whole book at once.

System Requirements (PC)
Intel Pentium processor
One of the following: Microsoft Windows 95 OSR 2.0, Windows 98 SE, Windows Millenium Edition, Windows NT 4.0 with Service Pack 5, Windows 2000, or Windows XP
64 MB of RAM

24 MB of available hard disk space

Additional 34 MB of hard disk space for PDF file (recommended)

Additional 70 MB of hard disk space for Asian fonts (optional)

System Requirements (Macintosh)

PowerPC processor

Mac OS 8.6*, 9.0.4, 9.1, or OS X*

64 MB of RAM

24 MB of available hard disk space

Additional 34 MB of hard disk space for PDF file (recommended)

Additional 70 MB of hard disk space for Asian fonts (optional)

(* Some features may not be available)

To Read the Guide (PC)

Insert the CD-ROM in your CD-ROM drive; a menu will appear on your screen. To read the guide, click on the "Get Wired" icon.

If you don't have Adobe Acrobat Reader installed, click on the icon that corresponds to your operating system (for example, "Adobe Reader Windows XP"). Follow the onscreen instructions, accepting all defaults, to automatically install the proper version of Adobe Acrobat Reader. Restart your computer before continuing.

To Read the Guide (Macintosh)

Insert the CD-ROM in your CD-ROM drive; an icon called "Wired by God" will appear on your desktop. Double-click the icon, and the disk will open. Double-click the file "Wired by God.pdf" to open the guide.

If you don't have Adobe Acrobat Reader installed, click on the icon that corresponds to your operating system (for example, "OS X 10.22-10.3"). If the folder contains another folder, drag it to your Applications folder and you're ready to go. If the folder contains an installer, then double-click the icon to install. Follow the onscreen instructions. Restart your computer only if the installer instructs you to do so.

Introduction:
Helping Teens Dream

Life is a great adventure, or nothing.
HELEN KELLER

To an aspiring tennis player, the dream is Wimbledon.

To a 260-pound, muscled-up linebacker, it's the Super Bowl.

To a perfectly pitched vocalist, it's the center stage on Broadway.

Whatever your teenager's dream, God has wired him or her for a unique future full of possibilities. You as a caring parent play a vital role in life's most fulfilling and rewarding arena—helping to shape that dream and make it come true.

To the Hauschild family in Oklahoma City, "dream building" is helping a 14-year-old daughter run a triathlon on one leg and one prosthesis, after bone cancer required amputation.

To one family in Missouri, dream building is helping their daughter publish and distribute 30,000 copies of a book she wrote at age four and illustrated at age seven—a book telling the world about her grandmother's heroic faith.

To the Foley family in Denver, the joy of dream building came as parents Steve and Cindy encouraged daughter Natalie after a disheartening fall—and watched her compete for a place on the world championship team and a chance to represent the United States of America.

To another family in Texas, dream building meant patching up the broken heart of their son, ridiculed for being big and clumsy—and launching him into Division I Big Ten football greatness.

Some parents, like a single mom in the Midwest, build dreams alone.

Arising before the sun comes up, she ferries her 17-year-old daughter in a minivan to a local swimming center and naps until dawn in the backseat. Then she works an eight-hour shift as a school nurse to get food on the table.

In orchestras, art shows, science fairs, basketball courts, and hockey arenas, insightful moms and dads are spending the greatest years of their lives developing their kids' God-given gifts and talents. They do it in a careful, hand-in-hand, side-by-side process that allows their teens to grow a dream from conception to celebration. Over mountains of acclaim, through lonely valleys of discouragement, and along winding trails of discovery, these dream builders and their dreamers travel one of life's most rewarding roads.

For these parent-teen teams, the "pot of gold at the end of the rainbow" is much more than a letter jacket, a state championship ring, a straight-A report card, or a perfectly executed piano recital. As good as those short-term fulfillments are, the never-ending satisfaction comes from building the parent-child relationship, teaching a valuable work ethic, and deepening your teen's faith as he or she explores ways to serve God.

After navigating that extraordinary highway with four teens of my own and assisting some 20,000 young dreamers each summer in our 10 sports camps, I can tell you this without a shadow of doubt: The time you, as a parent, invest in becoming a dream builder, helping your child discover his or her unique wiring, will be one of the most cherished investments you'll ever make.

Parents everywhere are doing that every day. You can, too.

—JOE WHITE

part one

getting
started

1

a house full of green lights

Until the big storm, Ed's parents encouraged him to pursue his dream of building a convertible out of Q-tips.

When Matt was little, his parents read to him daily from illustrated children's books. He developed a love of stories and art. By age eight he was writing his own epics, complete with drawings of the characters and action. Never mind that at that stage his people's arms and hands looked like flippers on a seal. He was hooked!

Mom and Dad read and praised every story, even the ones that were difficult to follow. They encouraged Matt's drawings with comments like "That's a great-looking spaceship!" and "Ooh, that bad guy really looks nasty! I'm glad he's not after me!" Matt continued to write—and especially to draw.

As the years went by, his drawing skills improved dramatically. Mom and Dad saw that his interest remained strong, and they supported it in any way they could. They bought drawing pads, special pencils and erasers, and instruction books. They faithfully attended every student art show and enthusiastically expressed their admiration for Matt's work. They planned family vacations to include scenic spots where he could sit for hours at a time and begin a new picture. (One day in Yellowstone National Park, Mom even held an umbrella over his head and sketch pad through two hours of light rain!)

By the time he got to high school, Matt was taking every art class available. When he worked on a picture, classmates would look over his shoulder and say things like "Did you really draw that?" and "You ought to frame that one!" Gradually, the dream of working and serving God in the field of art took root in his mind and heart.

Today Matt is in college, majoring in art. The future shape of his dream isn't clear yet, but he's hard at work, developing the skills and interests God gave him. Mom and Dad are still cheering him on, providing financial support, telling him how proud they are of the young man he's become, and helping him to discover and explore new possibilities.

Is your teen, like Matt, on the track to a meaningful future? Are you, like Matt's parents, finding out what a joy it can be to help a young person make the most of how God has wired him or her?

Since you've picked up this book and read this far, I believe you share my passion to help teens dream big, fulfilling, God-honoring dreams. But how, exactly, do we do that? That's what this book is all about.

Just Another Chore?

If you're thinking that raising a teenager is tough enough without having to turn yourself into a full-time guidance counselor, you're right. I know you're busy. You've already got more to-dos on your list than you're ready to handle. You want to provide the help your teen needs, but you're wondering where you'll find the time and energy to take on what sounds like another big responsibility.

Believe me, I've been there. My wife and I raised four highly active teens while directing multiple sports camps, leading Bible studies, and doing all the other parental running around that's required by modern life. Yet helping our teens to dream never felt like a chore. It was fun, exciting, and a natural part of coaching them through adolescence.

That can be your experience, too.

In this chapter and the next, I'll show you how to provide a home atmosphere that supports dreams and builds a teen with the confidence that those dreams can come true.

In Part Two, I'll guide you—and prepare you to guide your child— through the great experiment known as your teen. In all of human history, there's never been another person with your teen's exact mix of God-given personality, talents, interests, and spiritual gifts. As the two of you get to know that unique wiring through the self-tests in each chapter, you'll start to see which kinds of dreams might make a good fit.

In Part Three, I'll show you how to help your child put his or her plans in perspective. You'll aid your teen in learning to see where God is at work in the world, beginning to make today's choices in view of long-term goals, and gaining the most from life's hardest lessons.

Finally, in Part Four, I'll challenge you to pull together with your spouse if you're married, to give whatever it takes to help fulfill your teen's dreams, and to make sure the right dream—your child's—is being pursued.

Blue-Sky Thinking

No matter what we *say*, our children usually imitate what they see us *do*. If you're a dreamer, your teen is likely to be a dreamer. If you believe God has plans for using your time and talents, if you're serving Him regularly in your church and community, if you're open to things like short-term missions trips or even a change in careers as He might lead—your teen is apt to believe and do the same kinds of things.

This is an influence that no one but *you* (and your spouse, if you're married) as a parent can wield.

Have you stopped dreaming? That's easy to do when you're raising a family and established in a career—one that perhaps pays the bills but doesn't satisfy. It's easy to stop picturing and planning for a brighter future other than eventual retirement. It's easy to fall into a rut, a mind-set often labeled "being realistic." But if we do that, and stay stuck there, our children are likely to imitate us and to think and live in ruts as well.

If we want our teens to be dreamers—to picture and pursue a challenging and fulfilling future—we need to be (or become) blue-sky thinkers ourselves. We need to believe that whatever our lives have held so far, God isn't through with us yet. He still wants to work in and through us, to challenge us, and to bring us meaning by employing *our* unique blend of talents, gifts, and interests. If we believe that blue skies lie ahead—that life is still full of possibilities and opportunities provided by a loving heavenly Father—our teens will believe it, too.

Steve and Donna Thurman found out how true this is. The popular founding pastor and his wife of a large and growing church in Colorado, they might have stayed comfortably and indefinitely on the beautiful Front Range. God, however, had wired them differently and had a new dream for them.

As Steve explained in his sermon announcing their intention to leave, God made some people to be pioneers and others to be settlers. He and Donna were pioneers, he said, and God had been growing in them the dream of moving halfway around the world to help develop church leaders in the spiritually needy land of New Zealand. It was time for them to take the first steps of faith leading Down Under.

Years later, Steve and Donna can see how their willingness to dream and pursue big things for God affected their own teenagers: "Today our kids—the two youngest, anyway—are 'adventurers' by nature and by the fact that they've followed us around for over 20 years and seen that 'traveling light' and chasing dreams and taking risks are all 'the way to go.' 'What's the worst that can happen?' they tell us. Not much, except that you'll have some great memories and some stories to tell and some new friends you've met along the way. To the kids, God is big—a lot bigger than the fear of taking risks and making changes."

You don't have to become a missionary and move 8,000 miles to be a blue-sky thinker. But you do need to remain open to the possibility—and demonstrate it to your teen—that God may want to use you and your family in new and exciting ways in the future.

Support Your Teen's Interests

Another way to create a home full of green lights is to support your teen's interests—in academics, sports, music, church or community service, the arts, technology, cars, or whatever. This support takes the form of time (attending sporting events or science fairs, for example), effort (helping your teen practice the sport or build the science project), money (for lessons, supplies, and equipment), and encouragement. I'll say more about all of these in coming chapters, especially chapter 14, but for now let's focus on encouragement.

>> "My parents have encouraged me to pursue areas I'm interested in. They have told me my strengths and said why these would be helpful in the area I want to study. They've also had me be involved in different Christian services to be able to explore my gifts."
—Monica

Peers are not nice to each other. Many teens are catty; they cut and they gossip. They don't encourage each other to pursue meaningful goals. If a teen and her dreams are like a steam engine that needs to have coal shoveled into the boiler every day to keep running, peers are often coal thieves. They steal that source of energy with their snide, envious remarks. But we parents can supply every day the coal—true, sincere encouragement—that will fuel our teens' fire.

During the day, raided by negative coaching, negative teachers, negative peers, and a negative school environment, a kid runs out of coal. His little bank of confidence burns up. But a parent has a chance to spend the evening with a child. At the dinner table, out shooting baskets, helping with homework, before bed, the parent has lots of opportunities to praise.

Some parents assume their opinions no longer matter to their teens. It's true that peers are of great importance to teens as they establish their individuality and prepare for independence. But all teens—including yours—still long to be loved and affirmed by Mom and Dad. No one else's praise and support means more.

When it comes to encouragement, the more frequent and specific the better. That's why, at our Kanakuk football camps each summer, we make it our goal to encourage each teen by name 10 times a day. We want every kid to hear his name—and something specific that he's doing well—at least that often. Some of our kids will start in Division I, and some will never put on a helmet in a college game—but they all walk away from 26 days of Kanakuk feeling as if they can run through buildings. They love it!

If he's running the ropes—an agility drill—a camper will hear things like "Great job with your knees, Bill! Your eyes are up perfect! Great quick feet, Bill!"

A guy running sprints will hear "Way to sprint, John!" or "Super job, John! Man, I love the way you do your backwards run!"

Those things may sound tiny. But when a kid hears them 10 times or more a day, every day, with his name attached, he begins to believe in himself.

What works with adolescents at Kanakuk football camps will work with our teens at home. The more we encourage them, and the more specific our praises are, the more coal we'll provide for their boilers. If your teen is a budding artist, for instance, your comments might include things like "I love your way with colors, Mary!" or "That fruit in your picture looks so vivid, I'd like to grab it and take a bite, Kevin!" or "The combination of textures in your sculpture is fascinating, Sue! I could look at it over and over and see something different in it every day!"

A teen who gets that kind of encouragement will keep pursuing her dreams.

Encourage Your Teen to Try Different Things

Many young people have yet to zero in on a specific dream for the future. That's why Part Two of this book provides self-tests to help teens get a better handle on the way they're wired. But you don't have to wait to get started. One of the simplest—and most effective—ways to help teens is to encourage them to try a wide variety of activities:

- Does your son think he'd like to play the guitar? Rent an instrument, get him some lessons, and encourage him to work at it for at least six months.
- Does your daughter like to run? Buy her some good shoes and shorts, and encourage her to go out for the cross-country team.
- Does your son think he might like to work with children, maybe even become a teacher? Encourage him to volunteer with a Sunday school class at your church.
- Does the medical profession appeal to your daughter? Encourage her to volunteer at a local hospital and to interview your family doctor about "what it's really like."

Some of these efforts won't go so well, but that's okay. Your child may learn which interests *not* to pursue—an invaluable lesson. Other efforts will show promise, meriting further study and practice. Sooner or later, one may prove to be the most enjoyable and natural fit in the world.

We could call this the Ephesians 2:10 search: "For we are God's workmanship, created in Christ Jesus to do good works, which God prepared in advance for us to do." If God has prepared good works for our teens, then encouraging them to try different things will help them find areas of service for which the Lord has already wired them.

Say Yes

Another way to create a house full of green lights is to say yes as often as possible when your teen wants to try a new activity or take the next step in pursuing an interest. That sounds simple, but it's not.

For one thing, saying yes can be scary for a parent. If your teen hasn't enjoyed much success lately in drama tryouts or getting elected to student council, you might fear her heart will be broken again. If he wants to take up hockey, you might fear physical injury. Those are both legitimate concerns.

Your *yes* can also mean a commitment of your time, money, and energy. Say yes to an interest in art, for example, and you may be buying paints and pencils and sketch pads and canvases and lessons for a long time. Say yes to a sport like softball and you may be buying gloves and spikes and bats and other equipment for the next decade, not to mention taxiing your teen to a seemingly endless string of practices, games, and tournaments.

If at all possible, however, say yes to the things your teen wants to pursue. *Yes* is a door opener. It's a switch that turns on lightbulbs inside kids. It fires the imagination, stimulates creativity, and opens the door to a world of opportunities.

When my daughter Jamie was five years old, I told her about the idea of sponsoring a needy child in another country through a Christian ministry. I gave her a picture of a Cambodian child. Jamie thought about it, then asked if she could use her Christmas gift to begin supporting that child. My wife, Debbie Jo, and I said yes. Jamie put the picture on her bulletin board and developed a feeling of connection to that child.

A few years later, as a high schooler, Jamie started a clothing company (a story I'll tell in more detail later). She wanted to give any profits to help hurting children in the U.S. and abroad. Again Debbie Jo and I said yes. Jamie's company made $300,000 over the next several years—and Jamie did indeed give it all away! Hundreds of needy kids continue to benefit every year as a result.

Not every teen is going to start a business and generate that kind of income, of course. But saying yes to possibilities and passions, thereby sowing seeds of opportunity, applies to every parent and teen. As your young person explores gifts and talents and interests—whether that means taking piano lessons or joining a gymnastics team or helping to build a house with Habitat for Humanity—say yes whenever you can. Your teen will learn, and the dreams will grow.

Evaluate Setbacks: Learn, Grow, and Go

Here's one more way to provide a house full of green lights. It's helping our teens deal with the reality that setbacks are almost inevitable on the road to a dream.

The question isn't "Will glitches happen?" but "How should we respond when they do?" I'll say more about this in chapter 13, but for now let's note that the healthy response is to *learn, grow, and go.*

A setback might mean that a door is closed and the teen needs to look for another that's open. But it might also mean that God wants to develop perseverance, the ability to forgive, or some other character quality in the teen.

Is the setback a dead end or just a detour? Drawing on our experiences with God and with life, we can help our teens tell the difference. We can also help them learn lessons the situation has to teach.

As our young people struggle with the emotions and absorb those lessons, they can grow stronger and wiser—better prepared for future successes and losses. Some wisdom can't be gained in any other way, making setbacks one of God's most effective teaching tools.

Then, when they're ready, our teens can go on to the next opportunity—the next step in a dream that's still alive or the first step in a new one. Setbacks are part of life's journey of adventure.

That was true for Matt, the young artist introduced at the start of this chapter. When he entered a college art program that enrolled more students than it could train, he found the competition was tough. Professors tried to weed out those who lacked talent and motivation.

In one of Matt's early classes, he labored to please the instructor—sometimes without success. Finally, about midway through the semester, the teacher said, "Maybe you should consider transferring to another major."

Now, *there's* a setback in the pursuit of a dream! Many people might be crushed by such a comment. Matt could have concluded, "Surely this is a dead end, a blocked path."

But Matt believed God had given him a talent. He saw the comment as a bump in the road, not an impassable roadblock—a test of whether he could and would persevere.

He was determined to pass that test. When the next class time came a few days later, he was there with a portfolio of his best pre-college work, which he showed to the instructor.

The professor looked at drawing after drawing, his eyes growing wider with each one. Finally he closed the portfolio and told Matt with a smile, "I guess you belong here after all."

And the dream, birthed and nurtured in a house full of green lights, lived on.

// WITH YOUR TEENAGER

Over sundaes at your local ice cream shop, ask your teen a few questions like these:

- Is there anything new you've been thinking of trying—a sport, a musical instrument, the drama club? If so, how might I help you pursue that?

- If you were to choose today how you'd like the rest of your life to go, based on your interests and the things you feel you're good at, what would that look like?
- I'd like to be more of a "personal cheerleader" to you every day. What kinds of comments do you find especially encouraging?

2

building your teen's self-esteem

*Kaylia was glad employers couldn't sense her
low self-esteem during job interviews.*

Jared's parents love him; he's fairly sure of that, at least some of the time. But nothing he does is ever quite good enough for them. For as long as he can remember, their response to a 93 on a school paper has been, "Why didn't you get a 100?" Their response to his getting two hits in a baseball game is always, "Okay, you got two hits, but you struck out with the bases loaded in the sixth inning, didn't you? And you made that error in the seventh. So don't get the big head, Jared."

They don't need to worry about that. Thanks to their constant fault-finding and lack of affirmation, Jared's self-esteem is close to zero.

Others—teachers, friends, coaches, youth leaders—see Jared as bright and talented, with a world of potential. He sees himself as a failure. As far as he's concerned, he can't do anything well, and he never will.

Nancy's parents love her; she has no doubt. No matter how well she does or doesn't do in school, sports, or other activities, they clearly believe in her and support her. "You got an 89 on this chemistry test, Nance? Well, you've got a good head for science, so you'll start understanding it better soon. Tell you what: After dinner, let's go over the test and see what you can learn from your mistakes."

» " ' For I know the plans I have for you,' declares the LORD, 'plans to prosper you and not to harm you, plans to give you hope and a future.' "
—*Jeremiah 29:11*

"Yes, Nance, you lost your golf match, but remember you made that birdie with the long putt and saved par from the rough those two times. Your game has improved so much just since the start of this season, and we're so proud of how you hung in there even when you fell behind!"

Nancy's parents have a confident young lady in their home. Thanks to their steady encouragement and affirmation, her self-esteem is healthy. She's not arrogant, but she does believe in herself, and she has embraced the idea that God might want to use her life in significant ways.

As far as Nancy is concerned, God has wired her with potential, and the future is bright with possibilities that she intends to explore enthusiastically.

The Need for Healthy Self-Esteem

Healthy self-esteem helps teens to dream big. Confidence in God-given interests and talents and spiritual gifts, coupled with a sense of calling and mission as described in Ephesians 2:10, enables teens to seek and boldly pursue their passions.

Conversely, teens with low self-esteem—who believe they're not smart or talented or capable of much—lack the confidence that they can accomplish anything of significance. With faint hope of success, they'll dream small if at all—and dare little.

Notice that I'm talking about *healthy* self-esteem, not arrogance or egotism—"the big head" that concerns Jared's folks. I'm talking about teens who . . .

. . . know they were made in God's image and are of priceless worth to Him and to their parents.

. . . understand that God has wired them to have a unique-in-all-the-world blend of talents, personality, and passions.

. . . believe God has plans for them, to give them a meaningful future full of possibilities and hope (see Jeremiah 29:11).

So how do we parents build that kind of healthy self-esteem into our teens? Here are seven ways to do that.

#1: Show Unconditional Love

Remember what it was like to be a teenager? Remember the fragile ego, the desperate desire to be accepted and loved, feeling sky-high one moment and Death Valley-low the next, depending on how others treated you? That's exactly what your teen is going through now. Caught in this emotional turbulence, he needs more than almost anything else to know that his parents love him unconditionally.

> "My parents told me I could play college football, even when I never played in high school. They also told me they loved me whether I played none or a lot."
>
> —*Brent*

You may be thinking, "Of *course* I love my child, no matter *what* he does! Surely he *knows* that!"

I trust you really do love your teen that way. But the key question is, *does she understand and truly believe* that you love her without condition? Does she know that no matter how she acts, what she says, what choices she makes, how badly she frustrates you, or what kind of trouble she gets into, you will accept her as she is and love her completely?

In spite of our best intentions, it's easy to give the impression that our love is highly conditional—that we love our teens more or less depending on how they're doing in school, how they're performing in sports, how they look, who their friends are, or how "spiritual" they seem. Based on what we say, how we say it, and how we treat them, they can reasonably conclude that our love is far more fickle than firm.

That was certainly Jared's experience. After counseling thousands of adolescents over the past 30 years, I wish I could say that Jared is the rare exception. Unfortunately, he's in the middle of a crowd of today's teens who feel the same way.

Your teen may be one of them. As much as I love my kids, of all the personal battles I've had to fight in my lifetime, the struggle to squelch my overcritical spirit as a parent has been and remains one of the fiercest. Perhaps that's true of you as well.

Want to test how your love and acceptance of your teen might be coming across? Try recalling the last time you faced the following three situations. What did you say? What did you do? How did your teen respond? Most importantly, how do you think your teen may have interpreted your words and actions?

Situation 1: The last time your teen brought home a report card that included a grade you found disappointing.

Situation 2: The last time your teen was about to leave the house wearing clothes or makeup you didn't like.

Situation 3: The last time your teen competed in sports or took part in a play, concert, art show, or other public performance.

If you're like most of us, you probably said or did something that an insecure, already-had-a-bad-day teen could construe as meaning that she hadn't earned a full measure of your love:

"I told you turning in that paper late would cost you."

"No child of mine is going out in public looking like a bum!"

"Sure, you made a few baskets, but what about those turnovers you made that gave the other team easy fast breaks?"

"Maybe your brother could give you some tips on projecting your voice."

Want to do more to convey unconditional love? Here are some suggestions:

Say it, even if it seems obvious. It's impossible to say "I love you" too often. Say it when your teen does well or poorly, when she's happy or sad. Say it orally, in handwritten notes, in E-mails. Say it when you know she'll respond warmly, and say it when she's likely to mumble "Yeah, yeah." Say it when you're alone together, and say it in front of her friends (she may groan, but they'll be jealous).

Don't stop with words. All children, including teens, spell *love* like this: T-I-M-E. Love's reality is proved by your willingness to invest time in the relationship. Is your teen struggling with algebra? Don't just make sure he's spending an hour on it every night; sit down and help him work through the problems. Is she hurting because of an unkind remark from a friend? Don't just tell her time heals all wounds; take her out for ice cream and let her pour her heartache into your sympathetic ears.

Remember, too, that teens still need positive, loving touch from Mom and Dad—a hug, a kiss, a pat on the back or the knee, a shoulder rub at the end of a tough day. They may want you to "cool it" in front of their peers, but they still crave affirming, appropriate touch.

Don't save love for special occasions. Some parents save expressions of affection for times when kids have "earned" it by their behavior or accomplishments. These moms and dads think this will motivate teens to do even better. But a teen most needs to be reassured of your love when he's blown it—when he's failed the test, forgotten the line in the play, dropped the fourth-down pass at the end of the game, or gotten the traffic ticket.

Keep your teen's emotional tank full. An emotional "gas tank" fuels every child's journey through life and needs to be refilled regularly. That fuel consists of "I love yous," praise, compliments, positive touches, time, and attention—anything that expresses your love and affirms your teen's worth. Teens with full tanks find it much easier to dream big dreams and believe they can come true.

Hate the sin, but love the sinner. Your teen *will* do things that frustrate, disappoint, even hurt you. It's inevitable, because we're all sinners. When you need to administer discipline, how will you go about it? You can choose to convey condemnation ("How could you be so stupid? Do you realize what the other parents will think of me?") or love ("You knew better, didn't you? That's why I have to discipline you. But I love you so much, and I know you're going to learn a valuable lesson here").

Learn to accept yourself, too. Perhaps you have trouble expressing unconditional love to your teen because you struggle to love yourself in a healthy way. Remember that God loved you and gave the ultimate expression of that love before you ever thought of loving Him (see Romans 5:8). Remember that He's always with you and has plans for your success (see Joshua 1:9 and Jeremiah 29:11). Meditate on how much He loves you, and extend that same love to your teen.

#2: Demonstrate Grace

Grace keeps dreams alive. Condemnation kills them.

Grace is a gift, undeserved favor. It doesn't ignore wrongdoing, but it says, "I still love you. I forgive you. We're in this together, and I'm going to give you another chance to get things right." When differences over clothes or music or politics arise, grace says, "I love you, and our relationship is more important than anything we might disagree about."

Suppose Jared from our opening story comes home from school one day and admits, "Mom, I tried to make it through a changing traffic signal and got ticketed for running a red light." She might respond in one of these ways:

Response 1: "What? Haven't your father and I warned you about that a million times? How could you be so stupid? Do you have any idea what this will do to our insurance rates? Sometimes I think they must have switched you at birth with my real son, because no child of mine could be so irresponsible! Well, it's going to be a mighty cold day in July before you're allowed to drive again, young man!"

After that, how will Jared feel about himself?

Response 2: (after a hug, looking him in the eyes) "Oh, Jared, I'm glad you weren't hurt! But we've talked about what to do when a light turns yellow, and about the penalty for running a red light. No driving privileges for the next week. *(after a pause, smiling)* You're going to be driving for a lot of years, so you need to learn to do it safely now. I remember it took me a few fines—not to mention a fender bender—to learn my lessons as a teen driver."

What will Jared's self-esteem be like after that exchange?

A condemning response leaves a teen feeling worthless and alone. A gracious response leaves him feeling understood and valued, even when there's a penalty to be paid.

#3: Catch Them Doing Good

One day I visited the office of a successful businessman. On his desk I noticed a sign that said, "Every day, catch your child in the act of doing something good and tell him about it." The idea made a lot of sense and stuck in my mind.

I made it my goal—one of my diehard core values—that every day each of my children would hear his or her name with an encouraging word attached to it. That may sound like a minor assignment, but it's huge—because there are going to be times of tension and times when a child has to be corrected. But even on those days, one for-sure encouraging word, specifically attached to a positive accomplishment, goes gallons toward filling a kid's emotional gas tank.

It's easy to notice and react to things our teens do that annoy or frustrate us, like talking on the phone too long or playing music too loudly. We're quick to point out things they could have done better, like cleaning their rooms or writing a paper for school. But if critical comments are all they hear from us—or even if it just *seems* that way to them—their self-esteem and their capacity to dream will nosedive.

Don't know what to look for and praise in your teen? Here are a few ideas to get you started:

"I noticed you took out the garbage without having to be asked twice. Thanks!"

"I saw you helping your sister with her spelling. That was great!"

"You know, as hard as you work at staying in shape and improving your soccer skills, I'll bet you can succeed at just about anything you set your mind to."

"Hey, thanks for filling the gas tank before you brought the car home last night. I'd thought I would have to make time for that on my way to work this morning."

"Your room looks neater today. I'm impressed!"

"Mrs. Jones, your English teacher, told me you're her most-improved student this quarter. I'm so proud of you!"

Whether your compliments are large or small, they'll make their mark if they're sincere. Given day after day, they'll feed your teen's self-esteem and ability to dream.

#4: Help Them Find Areas of Success

High schooler Sarah views herself as average in every way—average looking, an average student, an average athlete, neither a part of the really popular group nor a social outcast. As far as she can see, there's nothing outstanding about her, and her present and future appear pretty unexciting.

Then one day she sees a sign on a school bulletin board announcing that the community center needs volunteers to work with autistic children. Sarah mentions it after school in response to Mom's "How did your day go?"

Mom, who's noticed that Sarah relates well to young cousins and neighborhood kids, suggests, "You might want to give that a try. I think you'd be good at it."

"Really?" Sarah asks. "Why do you think that?"

"Well," Mom replies, pausing to reflect for a moment, "do you remember how you were with little Jimmy down the street last summer? Everyone else thought he was just being a rebellious brat and tried to avoid him, but you played with him for a while and got him talking. You found out that this was the first time he'd ever moved into a new area, and he didn't know how to get attention in a positive way and make friends."

"Yeah, I remember," Sarah says, smiling.

"And after that you introduced him around, organized some games for all the kids, and practically turned him into the most popular kid in the neighborhood over the next two weeks!"

Sarah laughs. "Maybe I *would* be pretty good with those autistic children."

A few days later Sarah is volunteering at the community center. A few months after that, she tells her mom one night, "It's hard to see progress with autistic kids sometimes. But they seem to have accepted me, and the program director says I really have a way with them. I feel like I'm doing something useful. Maybe I should think about becoming a special needs teacher or a counselor—maybe even a child psychologist."

"Why not?" Mom answers with a smile and a hug.

#5: Be Their Biggest Fan

Who's your teen's biggest fan? You, I hope.

Do you celebrate your young person's every achievement, no matter how large or small? Whether they're basketball All-Americans, reporters on the school paper, or budding child counselors, our sons and daughters are the greatest "thems" there will ever be. Each of their successes should be recognized.

It's been said that life consists of a great number of small events and a small number of great events. A parent who celebrates both builds into a child confidence in the future. When a confident teen starts peeking over that continental divide between today and tomorrow, he'll do so with optimism and hope. Whether he's considering medicine or missionary service, car making or cabinetry, he'll do so with an attitude that says, "Hey, I've found success before, and I'll find success now."

As our four kids grew, Debbie Jo and I collected nine photo albums of their peak moments, made 12 highlight videos, and put 320 photos up in the house. Many of those pictures are on the "Peak Moments Wall" in our den, the White family hall of fame.

In addition, whenever one of the kids took part in an athletic event or other program, the whole family was there to watch. Afterward came a special dinner to relive the triumph or commiserate in the defeat. Either way, the teen was helped to feel like a champion in the family's eyes.

With dependable and enthusiastic fan support like that, teens will believe in themselves and in the possibility of dreams coming true.

#6: Say No When Necessary

It's true that we need to say yes to our teens' interests as often as possible. Sometimes, though, the proper answer to a request is no. If handled correctly, this can actually build self-esteem rather than tear it down.

As both a teen counselor and a parent, I've found that a child who never hears the word *no* can be as out of balance as one who never hears a *yes*. Spoiled kids don't appreciate life's benefits and achievements. It can do more harm than good to hand everything to kids on the proverbial silver platter. Solomon's advice on servants applies to children, too: "If a man pampers his servant from youth, he will bring grief in the end" (Proverbs 29:21).

It's okay to tell a teen, "No, we can't afford those $120 running shoes (or $400 camera or $100 Broadway theater tickets). But if you want to work for it, maybe mow some neighbors' yards while they're on vacation this summer, you might be able to earn the money." The things earned through one's own sweat tend to mean a lot more.

Likewise, it's healthy to say a firm *no* to some privilege, like driving, as a way to shape teen behavior. When clear rules are established beforehand and enforced consistently and fairly, those boundaries provide a sense of security. A teen who hears this kind of *no* might complain loud and long—but subconsciously she's thinking, *My parents love me and care enough about what happens to me to guard me from something they believe will harm me.*

#7: Talk About Dreams and Possibilities

A final way to build our teens' confidence is to speak often and positively about their potential. Talk in terms of dreams and possibilities. Even if you see yourself more as a settler than a pioneer, or if you believe life has not been too kind to you, you still need to picture a hopeful future for your teen.

Kids need to hear regularly statements like these:

"Your possibilities are as big as your imagination."

"You've got such a bright future!"

"If you really want to try ____, go for it! We're behind you all the way."

"What would you want to do with your life if you knew you couldn't fail? You really can't, you know, because for every door that closes there are 10 others you can try."

"There's no telling what you can do if you really apply yourself."

"At your age, almost anything is possible."

"You have the potential to make the world a much better place."

Our teens will feel better about themselves and their dreams when they're encouraged to see the future as bright and their options as wide open.

Happy Dreamers, Happy Dreams

A healthy self-image equals a healthy capacity to dream. It's as simple as that.

When we show our teens unconditional love, demonstrate grace, catch them doing good, help them find areas of success, are their biggest fans, and talk about dreams and possibilities, they will believe that the future—their future—is bright with opportunities to serve God in significant ways.

// WITH YOUR TEENAGER

Over a Saturday breakfast at your local pancake place, talk with your teen about the following:

- I hope you know beyond any doubt that I love you no matter what, but sometimes I wonder how well I communicate that. Are there ever times when I say or do something that makes you doubt my love? What might you want me to say or do differently?
- What activities do you think you do the best? How do you feel when you're doing them? How can I help you learn to do them even better?
- What's the nicest compliment anyone ever gave you? Why did that mean so much to you?

part two

the great experiment

>>

3

understanding and affirming your teen's basic bent

Justin's friends assured him that they called him "Snowflake" because he was one of a kind.

I'd come to this church to speak to its high school group, and I arrived a little after the service had already begun. Up on the stage, playing at ear-piercing level, was a teenage rock band. Its musicians had dyed, spiked hair and wore funky-looking clothes. Their lyrics expressed a Christian message, but they were yelling the words and playing their instruments so loud that it was just killing me.

Entering the auditorium from the back, I noticed four or five adults sitting in the last row. From their facial expressions and body language, I knew they shared my reaction to the band's performance.

One man to my left, however, was an exception. He was older, slightly balding, conservatively dressed. He looked as if his taste in Christian music might run to the Gaithers or Point of Grace. Yet his head bobbed and his foot tapped in a vain attempt to match the beat. I watched the man in amazement, thinking, *How can he stand that music?*

Just then he looked in my direction and saw that I was staring. Waving me over, he pointed to the lead singer in the band—the wildest critter in the whole group, with long, unkempt, dyed-white hair.

"That's my son!" the man shouted with a smile.

When it came to personal tastes, this man and his teenager were miles apart. Yet this dad plainly loved and took pride in his child.

There's a lesson in that man's example. When our teens are different from us in tastes or personality or habits, it's easy to be critical and skeptical about their prospects for future success. That's the opposite of a mindset that encourages the pursuit of God-honoring dreams.

Like the father in the church that day, we need to understand, respect, and work with the way our teens are wired.

Ironically, we can also struggle to accept a teen if he's *like* us—if we see in him our own character weaknesses or bad habits. Then our criticism is directed at trying to banish from our child those things we don't like about ourselves.

In both cases, we're attempting to remake him or her into our concept of the "perfect person." The result will be frustration and disappointment all around, and a teen who lacks the optimism and hope needed to dream big dreams for God's glory.

The Basic Bent

As family experts Gary Smalley and Dr. John Trent said in their book *The Two Sides of Love,* "Children seem to come fully equipped with a God-given personality bent, and even as adults, we tend to express our bent clearly. For example, Proverbs 22:6 is a familiar verse that reads, 'Train a child in the way he should go, and when he is old he will not turn from it.'

"In the original language of the Old Testament, that verse actually reads, 'Train up a child *according to his bent . . .*' "[1]

And as family counselor Dr. James Dobson cautioned, "You will not be able to redesign the basic personality with which your child was born. Some characteristics are genetically programmed, and they will always be there. . . . My advice to you is to accept, appreciate and cultivate the personality with which your . . . child is born."[2]

When Jesus trained His disciples, He did so with their unique wiring and maturity levels in mind. Notice what Mark 4:33 says: "With many similar parables Jesus spoke the word to them, *as much as they could understand*" (emphasis added). In other words, Jesus made the effort to get to know His disciples. He tailored His teaching to match their level of understanding.

How do we get to know our teens as the unique persons they are, in order to help them dream fitting dreams? The rest of this chapter provides a guide.

Ask—Then Listen, Listen, Listen

It's amazing what you can learn if you ask good questions. And it's amazing what a teen will tell you as a parent, *if* . . .

. . . he knows you love him.

. . . he's convinced your love is unconditional and you won't condemn him no matter what he says.

. . . he believes you're listening because you're really interested in what he has to say.

I'm going to assume that your relationship with your teen is such that she does believe you love her unconditionally. (If you need help in this area, read "Building a Strong Parent-Child Relationship" in Focus on the Family's *Parents' Guide to the Spiritual Mentoring of Teens* [Tyndale, 2001].) With the foundation of a strong relationship in place, what kinds of questions should you ask to get to know your teen better?

As you've probably discovered, it's not always easy to get a teen talking. But my friend and longtime youth worker J. David Stone taught me how to use a series of questions to get kids to open up. Start with a cognitive query, like, "What do you want from life right now?" Listen carefully to the response. Follow up with an emotional question, such as, "How do you feel about that?" After listening some more, pose a behavioral question: "What are you doing to get what you want?"

>> "My parents often told me that I was special, a unique gift from God, and that no one looked like me in the whole earth."

—*Heather*

I've found these questions to be amazingly effective. Try them when you're talking with your teen at bedtime, when she seems troubled, or when she approaches you with a problem.

Here are some questions you can use anytime to find out how God has wired your young person:

- "What really drives you?"
- "What's the most fun you've ever had helping someone else?"
- "What dreams do you think God has given you?"
- "What can you do that most people can't?"
- "What ability would you most like to develop? Why?"
- "If God hired you for a summer job, what would you hope it would be? Why?"

And this one from Doug Fields, a youth pastor: "If you could design a specific way to serve God and knew you wouldn't fail, what would you do?"

Remember that your purpose is to listen and learn, to better understand and appreciate your teen's uniqueness. This is not the time for lectures and advice. Figuratively speaking, you need to have big ears and a small mouth, tough skin and a tender heart.

Another way to learn by questioning is to talk with others in your teen's life: teachers, youth group leaders, coaches, school counselors, Scout leaders, Sunday school teachers, parents of close friends. Ask what they've observed about your child's likes and dislikes, interests and passions, abilities and aptitudes.

Often these people will confirm your own observations. Sometimes, though, they'll describe a side of your teen that you hadn't noticed—or offer an insight you'd overlooked. Both kinds of remarks can strengthen your understanding of your son or daughter.

Testing the Wiring

Personality assessments can help you understand your teen's basic bent too. Many such tests are available. Here's one you can use right now. It's adapted from *The Two Sides of Love,* by Gary Smalley and John Trent.[3]

You're about to see four lists of words and phrases. In each list, circle the words and phrases that describe your teen most of the time.

TYPE "L"

Takes charge	Bold
Determined	Purposeful
Assertive	Decision maker
Firm	Leader
Enterprising	Goal-driven
Competitive	Self-reliant
Enjoys challenges	Adventurous

TYPE "O"

Takes risks	Fun-loving
Visionary	Likes variety
Motivator	Enjoys change
Energetic	Creative
Very verbal	Group-oriented
Promoter	Mixes easily
Avoids details	Optimistic

TYPE "G"

Loyal	Adaptable
Nondemanding	Sympathetic
Even keel	Thoughtful
Avoids conflict	Nurturing
Enjoys routine	Patient
Dislikes change	Tolerant
Deep relationships	Good listener

TYPE "B"

Deliberate	Discerning
Controlled	Detailed
Reserved	Analytical
Predictable	Inquisitive
Practical	Precise
Orderly	Persistent
Factual	Scheduled

Now, under which type(s) did you circle the most words and phrases? Those indicate your teen's dominant personality type(s). The letters stand for Lion, Otter, Golden Retriever, and Beaver.

This is just one way of categorizing personalities, of course. But it can be a useful one. As Dr. John Trent explains, here are descriptions of these four temperaments:

> *Lions (High "L" People)*
> Lions are take-charge, assertive, go-for-it people. . . .
> They like leading and being in charge, even of you. . . .
> You rarely have to motivate Lions—just point them in a direc-
> tion. . . . When a Lion's strengths are pushed out of balance, they
> become too strong or assertive and insensitive in their words or
> actions. They can become so intent on a project that they communi-

cate that the project is more important than the people involved. But when a Lion's strengths are balanced with loving sensitivity, they make wonderful leaders, great friends, and some of the best parents.

Otters (High "O" People)

Otters love life and especially people. They're tremendous networkers. . . .

Otters usually aren't into details. In school, they often start their papers the night before (why hurry?). . . .

Like the Lions, their strengths can be pushed to an extreme. Their tendency to be late or to put off doing routine things needs to be balanced with responsibility and an understanding of the pressure their lateness puts on others. With some added structure, their sensitivity can be a tremendous asset, especially when they serve as a spiritual leader in a home or ministry.

Golden Retrievers (High "G" People)

Sensitive and caring, Golden Retrievers have difficulty saying no. They're compassionate, wonderful team players, and are very loyal and loving. They care about *individuals* and want everyone to feel included. They're adaptable and willing to go with the flow. While the Lion often challenges the status quo and suffers the consequences, Golden Retrievers watch others make mistakes and avoid them (thus avoiding the pain). . . .

When they're older, Golden Retrievers can be called on to "put out fires" and make those around them feel loved and accepted. But [they] can have their feelings easily hurt (they're not weak, just sensitive).

Beavers (High "B" People)

Beavers are detailed and organized. They do things "right." They tend to start, *and complete*, a few projects each year. . . .

Beavers have a way of mentally filing things so they can always find them. This inner filing system includes details and experiences. For example, they remember what you said precisely a year ago—and what you were wearing at the time.

They're very good at analyzing and taking things apart. But when their strengths are pushed to an extreme, they can be so good at it that they take people apart as well. There is no critic like a Beaver—and that includes how they view themselves. They set high standards and can be very hard on themselves if they don't reach those goals. Overall, however, Beavers are wonderful to have on a family or work team. They follow through, are predictable, and make lasting contributions.[4]

Has this little test given you a better understanding of your teen's basic bent? I hope so. For years Dr. Trent has used these four "animals" to picture a person's God-given strengths. If you'd like to go deeper than this short, hand-scored test, read *The Two Sides of Love* (Focus on the Family, 1990). Or go to www.leadingfromyourstrengths.com, where you'll find a more detailed online assessment created by Dr. Trent. This "Leading from Your Strengths" test (for which there is a charge) takes five to seven minutes to complete; then you'll receive an insightful, E-mailed, 19-page word picture of your teen's unique qualities.

"But I already *know* my teenager's personality," you might be saying. "He's scatterbrained and never finishes anything. I don't see how he's ever going to set goals, much less reach them."

Believe it or not, the things you see as weaknesses in your teen's bent might turn into strengths—if brought under a little self-discipline and control. It may also help if you see those traits in a more positive light. Here's a list of personality minuses that could become pluses with your assistance:

Tone Down This Weakness	*Discover This Strength*
Critical	Analytical
Insincere	Appreciative
Domineering	Assertive
Overtalkative	Communicative
Worrying	Concerned

Tone Down This Weakness	Discover This Strength
Self-sufficient	Confident
"Know-it-all"	Counseling
Reckless	Courageous
Nosey	Curious
Stubborn	Determined
Weak-willed	Diplomatic, Tactful
Rigid	Effective
Flattering	Encouraging
Flowery	Expressive
Overly lenient	Forgiving
Wasteful	Generous
Daydreaming	Imaginative
Uncommunicative	Listening
Idolizing	Loyal
Judgmental	Moral
Overdependent	Obedient
Indecisive	Open-minded
Unrealistic	Optimistic
Perfectionistic	Orderly
Oversensitive	Sensitive
Undisciplined	Spontaneous
Dull	Stable
Harsh	Straightforward
Stingy	Thrifty
Fainthearted	Tolerant

Giving Your Blessing

Understanding your teen's personality is just one step toward helping him dream. The next is *affirming* him, personality and all.

God the Father said of Jesus, "This is my Son, whom I love; with him

I am well pleased" (Matthew 3:17). Our teens need to know we're pleased with them—whether or not their wiring is like our own. Armed with that approval—that blessing—they're more likely to be great dreamers.

How do we give our teens such a blessing? As John Trent explains in his book *The Blessing* (Thomas Nelson, 2004), there are five basic elements to conveying a blessing:

1. *Meaningful touch.* When our kids are young, it's easy to bless them with an embrace or a stroke of the hair. But when they become teens, many parents back off—especially fathers who are uncomfortable touching their maturing daughters. The simple truth, however, is that kids *never* outgrow their need for appropriate physical affection from Mom *and* Dad, even if they cringe outwardly at a public hug.

Even a handshake, a pat on the back, or a hand on the shoulder makes a powerful statement of affection and acceptance. If you want to bless your teen, relearn how to touch simply, briefly, appropriately. Both of you will benefit!

2. *Spoken words.* Out-loud affirmations are, unfortunately, few and far between in many homes. Sometimes it's because of parent-teen conflict. Other times it's due to parental concern about overinflating a teen's ego. And sometimes it's simply because Mom or Dad doesn't know what to say. Yet your words of blessing have tremendous power to build your teen's confidence and self-acceptance.

As Dr. Trent puts it, "Spoken words of blessing should start in the delivery room and continue throughout life."

3. *Expressing high value.* Those spoken words should make it clear that your teen is worth a lot—and that her value is based on who she is, not on what she can do. The parents of a physically challenged teen, for instance, tell her that no matter what she does or doesn't accomplish, she's their "claim to fame." The parents of a hyperactive teen tell him, "With all that energy and your different way of looking at things, you could be the next Bill Gates!"

Expressing high value can be especially potent during times of conflict.

Let's say you've been butting heads with your daughter over her choices in music. If, in the midst of that tension, you can tell her, "You know, you're still the best thing that's ever happened to your dad and me, in spite of our differences," the impact on your relationship—and on her ability to keep dreaming big things for her future—can be huge.

4. *Picturing a special future.* Kids take to heart comments like these, especially if they've been hearing them all their lives:

- "You're so lazy, you'll never amount to anything."
- "Don't sign up for that tough math class; it's only for smart kids."
- "Who's ever going to want to date, let alone marry, a fat slob like you?"

The good news is that our teens will also take to heart comments like these:

- "When I see you giving your best effort, I know you'll be able to do most anything you set your mind to."
- "Someday some lucky person is going to fall hopelessly in love with your beautiful spirit."

What kind of future is your teen picturing, based on what you've said to him over the years? If you're not sure, ask him! If the answer isn't what you want it to be, start today to paint a brighter picture with your words.

5. *Active commitment.* Blessing your teen as a unique individual includes devoting time, energy, creativity, and resources to know, train for, and support his or her hopes.

Do you know what makes her tick? Do you willingly invest time and resources to help her develop skills and pursue passions? Would she identify you as her biggest fan? Would she say that no matter what happens, she knows she can count on you?

If your honest answer to any of those questions is no, it's time to activate that commitment.

Has reading about these five elements made you feel a little inadequate? You've got lots of company! All of us parents can do better. The great news is that with God's help, we can start today to make positive changes—to get better at blessing our teens, personality and all.

The Great Experiment

In all of human history, there's never been another person quite like your teen. Part of his makeup comes from your genetic contribution; part from his other parent's; and part from the hand of God as He knit your child "fearfully and wonderfully" in his mother's womb.

It's as if God decided to conduct a great experiment. For one time only, He brought together this particular combination of genes and environment and divine stamp.

In the chapters to come you'll learn more about what makes your teen the individual he is. Your appreciation for his unique wiring will grow. So will your ability to help him dream about all God wants to do in and through him for the rest of his one-of-a-kind life.

// WITH YOUR TEENAGER

Over steaming cups at your local java joint, try the following:

- Ask: "What are some of the ways you've noticed that you and I are alike? What are some of the ways that we're different?"
- If your teen hasn't already done so, have him take the personality test included in this chapter (it's also included in the accompanying teen guide on CD-ROM). Compare his self-test results with your assessment of his personality.
- Ask: "Is there any part of your personality that you don't like? If so, what is it?" Use this chapter's list of weaknesses that can be turned into strengths to help answer this question: "If you could get that more under control, how might it become a strength for you?" Try to give an example of how you've turned a liability of your own into an asset.

4

helping your teen find interests and passions

Wesley felt sure that his fondness for doughnuts would qualify him for a career in tire sales.

Like many preteens, Greg had no particular passions that might develop into a career and a way of serving God. His parents encouraged him to try different things, though—and when he was about 13, he found his niche.

He discovered the world of stage productions. Drawn to the technical side of live performances—running a spotlight, working on a sound board—he looked for opportunities to acquire those skills.

His parents got behind this new interest. That meant driving Greg to and from play rehearsals and performances, arriving early and staying late.

The more Greg pursued this interest, the more he liked it. Before long his teachers, coaches, directors, and other tech people affirmed that he was good at it too.

Eventually Greg's passion became a career and a way to serve God. Today, through his own company, he produces and directs videos and films and provides TV and video services for live events put on by Christian ministries like Promise Keepers and the Smalley Relationship Center.

Says Greg, "As a parent now myself, I realize [my folks] gave sacrificially of their time to enable me to pursue this interest."

Greg's mom and dad certainly deserve credit for that. They used a pretty tough method of finding out what Greg's interests might be; we could call it the "hit or miss" approach. In this chapter, I'd like to introduce you to a different method that may save you some time as you zero in on your teen's interests and abilities.

Passions: Worth Pursuing?

Before I explain the method, however, let's talk motive. Is pursuing our interests and dreams a worthy goal for a Christian? Should we be encouraging our teens to find careers and other activities that intrigue them, or is that somehow selfish?

I believe God generally wants His people to pursue dreams and do related work that they find interesting and even feel passionate about. He's not a celestial killjoy who takes pleasure in seeing us suffer day after day in jobs that we hate, that don't interest us or challenge us or give us a sense of accomplishment. Instead, He takes pleasure in seeing us do work that fits the way He wired us.

Psychologist Clyde Narramore put it this way: "God generally calls a person into a field of employment in which he is spontaneously interested.

. . . God knows your interests and desires. He has influenced your past experiences and He wants you in the place where you will be happiest and most productive. Because of this He uses your interests to guide you into the right profession."[1]

Or, as Richard Bolles, author of the perennial bestseller *What Color Is Your Parachute?*, puts it, God wants us to enjoy doing well work that honors Him. So "when we use the talents He most wants us to use, that is our time of greatest joy."[2]

Career counselor John William Zehring wrote, "You can expect to be happy in your job if you have sought to understand yourself—your interests, potential, personality, and motivation. . . . When we apply the teachings of the Bible [e.g., Ecclesiastes 3:12-13; John 10:10] to that very complex business of career decisions, it is evident that God does not want us to do something which we are not interested in or where we are not happy."[3]

With that understanding, I present the following tool for helping your teen pinpoint interests, passions, and natural abilities. It was developed by Tim Sanford, a counselor at Focus on the Family who works with many teens. He calls it "The Vision Quest." A copy of it can also be found in the CD-ROM companion guide for teens.

The Vision Quest collects data from your teen's experiences to help determine his interests, ambitions, and goals. Like any assessment tool, it's not a final authority or an absolute answer. But it can help with the question "What do I want to be when I grow up?"

It's important to take your time with the Vision Quest. Just collecting your teen's experiences might take a few weeks, so don't rush.

Now here's the actual tool for your teen to use.

>> "My parents let me try ballet, gymnastics, cheerleading, and encouraged me in all opportunities that came up as a way to find out what I liked."

—Leslie

• • • _____

THE VISION QUEST

Here's a tool to help you pinpoint your interests and natural abilities. It was developed by Tim Sanford, a counselor at Focus on the Family who works with a lot of young people. He calls it "The Vision Quest." This isn't a final authority or an absolute answer. It's just a way to sort through your past and find clues to your future.

You'll need to make a few photocopies of the Vision Quest Worksheet, since you probably won't be able to fit everything on a single copy. And be warned that this isn't an exercise you can breeze through in 10 minutes. Take your time; we're talking about your future here!

1. On a piece of paper, list the things you've done since the fourth grade. We're talking about things like these:

   School: academics, sports, social events, performing arts, student government.

   Home: hobbies, interaction with family and friends, personal adventures.

   Church: youth activities, socials, special events, camps, worship, leadership, volunteer work, mission trips, "helping out."

   Community: scouting, clubs, sports, the arts, service projects.

   Work: job duties, volunteer or assigned tasks, chores.

   You don't have to compile your whole list at once. Allow two or three weeks, adding to it as new memories come to mind. If you don't know whether to include something in the list, go ahead and put it down anyway.

2. Make a few photocopies of the Vision Quest Worksheet.

3. In the center column of the worksheet, write each of the activities you listed in step 1 in chronological order according to the year they happened.

4. Now give each activity a "positive" or a "negative" rating. How did it turn out? How did it affect you? Look at the example at the top of the worksheet. Here are some ratings you can use:

-5 = total disaster	+5 = outstanding
-4 = really bad	+4 = excellent
-3 = bad	+3 = very good
-2 = disappointing	+2 = good
-1 = not good or bad	+1 = okay

There are no "right answers" here; your ratings are based on your feelings and opinions. You may want to change some of your ratings later; feel free, but use a different-colored ink so that you can remember both numbers.

VISION QUEST WORKSHEET

-5	-4	-3	-2	-1	EVENT (List chronologically and divide by year)	1	2	3	4	5
		NEGATIVE						POSITIVE		
					EXAMPLE: 2001					
					Helped with VBS					X
					Student council			X		
		X			Sang in choir					

5. Put the completed Vision Quest Worksheet away for three or four days and don't look at it at all. That gives your mind time to clear. Meanwhile, ask God to open your heart and mind to what He wants to show you. Don't try to rush the process. This is a quest, not a race.

6. After several days, pull your worksheet out and think again about the events to which you gave a negative value. Ask yourself if there were any factors that might have made those events seem more negative than they otherwise would have (moving, parents separating, major accident or illness, youth pastor change, etc.). This doesn't mean you have to change your rating; just make a note about how those factors might have influenced you.

7. Staying on the negative side of the worksheet, look for patterns. For example, if events connected with mechanical things (fixing the car, building something, helping with props at the school play) consistently ended in disaster, you're probably not the mechanical type. If this is true, accept it. Learning what you're not good at is as important as learning what you are good at.

   If all or most of your events are on the negative side, maybe you're overly tired or discouraged. You might not be evaluating yourself accurately right now. Put this exercise aside for a while and come back to it later. Talk things over with a parent, a mature friend, or another trusted adult. See if that person can help you see things more clearly. On the other hand, having only positive ratings may mean you're not seeing things clearly, too. Be honest with yourself.

8. Now move to the positive side of the worksheet. Highlight all the events that you marked with a +3 or higher. Ask yourself the questions below as you look over those highlighted events. Then feel free to add your own questions. The more questions you ask yourself, the more effective this exercise will be.
   - "Is there a pattern or anything these events have in common?"
   - "Are some of the activities things I'd like to pursue more?"
   - "How can I begin doing more of these kinds of activities?"
   - "What kinds of qualities, talents, character traits, and skills do these activities require?"
   - "Do I have some of those qualities and traits?"
   - "Are any circumstances or events missing from my worksheet? If so, what are they, and why might they be missing?"
   - "Are there any activities that I've never done before, but I'd like to try?"

9. Next, ask the same questions about all the remaining events you listed on the positive side of the worksheet.

10. Put the completed worksheet away again for several days. This gives your mind a second time to clear. Ask God again to open your heart to what He wants to show you. Remember, this is not a race.

11. Pull out the worksheet again and look it over briefly to see if anything new jumps out at you. If so, make a note of it. What conclusions can you draw? What things do you do well? What things do you not do well? It's important to look closely at the things you do well and that you enjoy doing.

God has made you "fearfully and wonderfully" (Psalm 139:14). Vision Quest is a great way to help you begin to discover how He's made you.

• • •

Questions That Encourage Dreaming

In addition to working through the Vision Quest together, try asking your teen questions like the following. You might want to ask them every six months or so, as interests and passions may change over time.

1. If you could do anything you wanted and knew you wouldn't fail, what would you choose to do, and why?

2. If you knew you had only two years to live, what would you want to do with that time?

The first question encourages your teen to think and dream boldly. If fear of failure and embarrassment are removed from the equation, with success guaranteed, what desire would she want to pursue with all her heart?

The second question isn't meant to be morbid or frightening. Rather, it challenges a teen's assumption that he'll live forever, helping him to consider what's really most important to him—and to God.

The Wiring Diagram

Are you gaining a sense of the way God has wired your teen? We're just getting started.

In the previous chapter we looked at your teen's unique personality. In this chapter we've considered his interests and passions. In the next we'll talk about his spiritual gifts.

In the process, I hope you'll begin to see the outlines of some God-honoring dreams your teen might develop—and some ways in which you can help make those dreams come true.

// WITH YOUR TEENAGER

Over homemade fruit smoothies at the kitchen table, try the following:

- If your teen hasn't already done so, have him fill out a "first draft" of the Vision Quest included in this chapter.
- Ask: "Did going through this exercise bring back good memories of some positive experiences? If so, what were they? What made them so positive for you?" (If your teen has trouble coming up with ideas, try to suggest some experiences you remember as positive.)
- Say: "You'll probably want to add to and change your list of experiences over the next few weeks. But can you see any patterns emerging, any things you might be good at or not so good at? Does anything stand out as something you'd like to try more of?"

5

discerning your teen's spiritual gifts

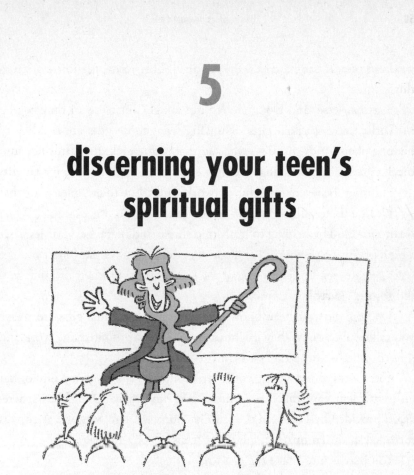

*Dean's claim that he had the gift of prophecy was
met with skepticism by others in the youth group.*

Katrina is 16. She has good grades in science and a strong interest in the workings of the human body. This year she's discovered she has the spiritual gift of service. Not surprisingly, her dream is to become a doctor and ease the suffering of others.

Jesse is 15. He's good with words and has received the spiritual gift of teaching. He decides to pursue the dream of becoming a Christian writer.

Doug is 18. He believes his primary spiritual gift is service. He hasn't picked a career path yet, but he likes setting up the room and the sound system for his campus group's Friday night worship service. He was also one of the hardest workers on a short-term mission construction project.

Katrina, Jesse, and Doug aren't unusual. *All* our teens, if they belong to Christ, have spiritual gifts. Knowing what those gifts are is a key to making plans for the future—whether that future includes pastoring, auto mechanics, or homemaking. We may be used to thinking of spiritual gifts as equipping believers for "church work" only, but there's plenty of that work to be done outside church walls. Take Katrina, for example. Won't she honor God by helping to heal strep throat and hiatal hernias? Jesus set a high priority on giving aid and comfort to hurting people: "I tell you the truth, whatever you did for one of the least of these brothers of mine, you did for me" (Matthew 25:40).

Do you and your teen know what his or her spiritual gifts are? Have you talked about how they might fit into a lifetime of satisfying work and service, whether full-time, part-time, or spare-time?

You can start discovering your teen's spiritual gifts by giving him or her an assessment tool called a spiritual gifts inventory. One follows here, again provided by Focus on the Family counselor Tim Sanford. A copy is included in the companion guide for teens on CD-ROM.

You may want to take the test too.

● ● ● ——————————————————————————————————

SPIRITUAL GIFTS INVENTORY

A spiritual gift isn't a natural ability with which you're born. It's not an office, position, or job you may hold. It's not a talent for dealing with people of certain ages.

Spiritual gifts are abilities that allow you to perform specific tasks beyond the realm of human skill. They're given to believers in Jesus Christ only, and they're given as gifts—not as a result of your maturity level, prayer, or education.

Whether all spiritual gifts mentioned in the Bible are still available today is a controversial issue. But it's generally agreed that every Christian has at least one spiritual gift. It's up to you to discover, develop, and exercise it.

Understanding your spiritual gifting has several phases. Begin by praying to understand the gift(s) the Holy Spirit has already placed inside you. You don't ask for a gift; you ask to be made aware of it.

Next, learn by doing. Get involved in situations where you have to depend on God's Spirit to get something done. Work on projects inside and outside your church. As you do, get ongoing, honest feedback from spiritually mature friends and leaders. Make an appointment with your youth pastor, a coach, or a teacher who knows you well, and ask what gifts that person sees in you.

There's no "complete" list of spiritual gifts, but partial lists are found six times in the New Testament. You may want to read these passages to get an overview of the gifts mentioned and their purposes in God's church today:

- Romans 12:6-8
- 1 Corinthians 12:4-11
- 1 Corinthians 12:28
- 1 Corinthians 12:29-30
- Ephesians 4:11-13
- 1 Peter 4:10-11

A great way to start discovering your spiritual gifts is to take a test called a spiritual gifts inventory. Here's one based on an exam by Focus on the Family counselor Tim Sanford.

Work through all seven lists. Mark with an "XX" any statements that seem to fit you well. Mark with a single "X" the statements you think may fit you.

Some of the statements have a negative tone. Those don't describe the gift itself but, rather, the personality of someone in whom that gift is often found.

When you've gone through all seven lists, add up the statements you marked on each list and enter that number at the end of the list. Give yourself one point for each statement, whether you marked it "XX" or only "X." Next, figure out the approximate percentage of statements marked on each list.

You'll probably find that one or two lists have more statements marked than the others do. Those lists may indicate your spiritual gift(s). Don't be surprised if more than one list has lots of marks. You may have what's called a primary gift and a secondary one.

LIST ONE

_____ You're very good at stating the truth, whether speaking or singing it.

_____ You're bold when you relate to others—maybe even frightening at times.

_____ You talk straight, and your standards are straight.

_____ You tend to use Scripture to back up what you say.

_____ You often can identify what's evil.

_____ You're able to tell a lot about people's motives and character.

_____ You want to confront other people's selfishness and stop it.

_____ When others say they've changed, you want to see proof—not just words.

_____ You're direct, honest, and persuasive.

_____ Feelings don't matter as much to you as choices, facts, and truth do.

_____ You'd rather confront than just "relate."

_____ You tend to be better at talking than listening.

_____ You want to proclaim truth and let people know what will happen if they reject it.

_____ You don't compromise with sin.

_____ You have a strong sense of who you are.

_____ You have a strong sense of duty.

_____ You're concerned that people respect God and understand His character.

_____ You don't particularly care what others think of you.

_____ You have strong opinions, and you may be stubborn.

_____ You're willing to be the "underdog."

_____ You can't stand it when people don't practice what they preach.

_____ You're more likely to be depressed than lighthearted about life and its problems.

_____ **Total number of statements you marked out of 22**

_____ **Percentage of statements marked**

LIST TWO

_____ You really want to meet people's physical needs.

_____ You understand the practical needs of individuals and the church.

_____ You can recall people's specific likes and dislikes.

_____ You care about the details of what needs to be done.

_____ You find it hard to say no when something needs to be done.

_____ You tend to get involved in too many things.

_____ In focusing on others' physical needs, you may overlook their deeper needs.

_____ You expect everyone to be as dedicated and energetic as you are.

_____ You want to get the job over with so you can get on to the next one.

_____ You want your help to be sincerely appreciated, and you can tell when a "thank you" isn't heartfelt.

_____ You're preoccupied with the goal in front of you.

_____ You have a lot of physical stamina.

_____ You're willing to sacrifice, and you want to get others to do that, too.

_____ You're often more concerned about getting things done than about getting along with others.

_____ You tend to have a low self-image.

_____ When you run out of time, you're frustrated because you can't do that extra little bit.

_____ You're usually easygoing.

_____ You're loyal.

_____ You listen to others without criticizing them.

_____ You don't talk a lot in public.

_____ You're comfortable with letting others be in charge.

_____ You can put up with people who might irritate others.

_____ **Total number of statements you marked out of 22**

_____ **Percentage of statements marked**

LIST THREE

_____ You're good at communicating in an organized way.

_____ You like helping others to learn.

_____ You insist on using words accurately.

_____ You like arranging facts in a simple way so others can remember them.

_____ You believe that without teaching, the Christian faith would fall apart.

_____ You like to quote the Bible and other sources to support what you say.

_____ You tend to be more theoretical than practical.

_____ You really love learning and studying.

_____ You test the knowledge of those who teach you.

_____ You have to know the source before accepting new information.

_____ You resist using Bible verses or stories in ways they weren't meant to be used.

_____ It's easy for you to become proud of your knowledge and insight.

_____ You do your own investigating to find out what's true.

_____ If you're teaching, you sometimes rely on your own ability instead of on God's help.

_____ You'd rather analyze information than relate to people.

_____ You're creative and imaginative.

_____ You're more objective (facts, figures) than subjective (feelings).

_____ You like researching truth more than presenting it.

_____ You're self-disciplined.

_____ You explain things with authority.

_____ You make decisions based on facts.

_____ You tend to talk more than listen.

_____ **Total number of statements you marked out of 22**

_____ **Percentage of statements marked**

LIST FOUR

_____ Nearly everything you do is practical.

_____ You get painfully bored hearing about theories.

_____ You really believe that what's humanly impossible is possible with God.

_____ You can visualize what a person could become through God's love.

_____ You love having conversations that help you see things in a new way.

_____ You tend to see trouble as a chance to grow.

_____ You really want your listeners to accept you and to approve of what you say.

_____ You like helping others solve their problems.

_____ You sometimes quote Bible verses out of context to make your point.

_____ You keep trying to make your point as long as others listen.

_____ You aren't satisfied until you've shown how to live out a truth in everyday life.

_____ It's hard for you to accept failure.

_____ You may write off those who cause you to fail.

_____ You find success exciting.

_____ You tend to give people advice instead of just befriending them.

_____ You tend to care more about getting results than about the other person's felt needs.

_____ You usually find it easy to talk in a group.

_____ You're more impulsive than self-disciplined.

_____ You're able to emotionally identify with others.

_____ You're more subjective (feelings) than objective (facts, figures).

_____ You tend to avoid formal ways of doing things if you don't see the point.

_____ You're motivated by a positive reaction from your audience.

_____ **Total number of statements you marked out of 22**

_____ **Percentage of statements marked**

LIST FIVE

_____ You insist that people follow the rules.

_____ You sometimes make enemies when others think you're "using" people.

_____ You're confident.

_____ You're comfortable being a leader.

_____ You know how to delegate work to others.

_____ You can see the overall picture and long-range goals.

_____ You tend to wait on the sidelines until those in charge turn over the responsibility to you.

_____ You're good at organizing.

_____ You're able to sit quietly and listen before making comments.

_____ You're eager to complete a task quickly and get on to the next one.

_____ You'll put up with criticism from those you work with in order to reach your goal.

_____ You thrive on pressure—the more the better.

_____ You sometimes get so caught up in getting things done that you aren't sensitive to others' feelings.

_____ You like seeing the pieces of a plan come together.

_____ You're tempted to get back at others who treat you badly.

_____ You're good at details.

_____ You're thorough and careful.

_____ You make decisions based on facts.

_____ You care more about what's good for the group than you do about your own desires.

_____ You're more composed than nervous.

_____ You tend to accept others based on loyalty or ability to finish a task.

_____ You're more objective (facts, figures) than subjective (feelings).

_____ **Total number of statements you marked out of 22**

_____ **Percentage of statements marked**

LIST SIX

_____ You give regularly and even sacrificially to your church and other ministries, no matter how much money you have.

_____ You make wise purchases and investments.

_____ You really believe in certain organizations that are trying to serve God.

_____ You want to have an active part in any cause to which you give.

_____ You carefully examine requests for your money.

_____ You want what you give to be of high quality.

_____ You refuse to be pressured into giving.

_____ You want your giving to motivate others to give.

_____ You want to avoid public recognition and give quietly.

_____ You want God to lead you in your giving.

_____ You get very upset when seeing others waste money.

_____ You're happy, even eager, to give.

_____ You make do with less in order to give quality to others.

_____ You may be good at earning money.

_____ You want confirmation by others you trust before giving.

_____ Your first thought when people ask for money is often "No."

_____ You have a pretty accurate view of yourself.

_____ You're more lighthearted than downhearted.

_____ You want people to like you.

_____ You're responsible.

_____ You love it when your gift is an answer to a person's prayers.

_____ You tend to be sympathetic.

_____ **Total number of statements you marked out of 22**

_____ **Percentage of statements marked**

LIST SEVEN

_____ You're very sensitive to others' feelings.

_____ Your feelings can be easily hurt.

_____ You're very interested in people.

_____ You're drawn to people who are in distress.

_____ Healing and prayer are important to you.

_____ You're deeply concerned about people's inner struggles.

_____ You'll go to great lengths to help others.

_____ You find it tough to be firm with others.

_____ You tend to ignore those who don't have obvious needs.

_____ You have a hard time trusting others for fear of being hurt.

_____ You're tender and kind, and you often express that by touching.

_____ You sacrifice to lessen others' pain and suffering.

_____ You can tell when you meet a person who's a "kindred spirit."

_____ You're turned off by people who aren't sensitive.

_____ You care more about feelings than facts.

_____ It's easy for you to get discouraged and say, "Poor me."

_____ You're inclined to have a low self-image.

_____ You're patient.

_____ You talk well with people, and they find it easy to talk to you.

_____ You can tell whether others are sincere.

_____ You're more subjective (feelings) than objective (facts, figures).

_____ When it comes to getting along with others, you can put up with a lot.

_____ **Total number of statements you marked out of 22**

_____ **Percentage of statements marked**

Now take a look at the test you just took. Does one list have more marks than the others? If so, that may be your primary spiritual gift. Does a second list stand out above the remaining five? That may be a "secondary" gift.

If no list stands out, look over all the descriptions and see if one seems to fit you better than the rest. Keep in mind that other issues, including stress, may block your ability to see a spiritual gift—and could block a gift from being displayed at all. Or your gift(s) may not be among those listed here. So be patient, and come back to this exercise later if necessary.

This test looks for what have been called the "seven motivational gifts" in Romans 12:3-9. Here they are:

LIST ONE: PROPHECY

If you have the gift of prophecy, you're probably highly sensitive to sin, to others' motivations, and to whether they're okay spiritually. This may not be too noticeable now, but it can become clearer as you mature. Being a prophet doesn't mean you have to hear God's audible voice talking to you; it means you're able to understand God's message and who needs to hear it.

LIST TWO: SERVICE

If you have the gift of service, you want to take care of the practical, physical needs of others. You're good at identifying unmet needs and helping church leaders meet them.

LIST THREE: TEACHING

With this gift, you have a passion for the truth and tend to make it clearer for others. You can communicate important information as a teacher or coach.

LIST FOUR: EXHORTATION

People with this gift are often seen as the encouragers or cheerleaders of a group. You can bring comfort and counsel to others.

LIST FIVE: ADMINISTRATION

If you have this gift, you like getting people to work together toward a goal. When you and your friends are planning a major activity, you're likely the one who gets everyone and everything organized—even if your friends think you're a little bossy in the process.

LIST SIX: GIVING
Yes, this is a real gift—though it often doesn't surface until a person is middle-aged. If you have this gift, you actually enjoy helping other people by giving away your money, possessions, and other resources. If you're secretly wanting this gift in the hope that God will make you rich so you can give part of your money away, you probably don't have the gift.

LIST SEVEN: MERCY
The gift of mercy is not "feeling sorry" for people. If you have this gift, you have a strong desire to heal physical and/or emotional wounds. You feel compassion for hurting people, and you translate that into actions that show love and relieve suffering.

Other gifts may fall under the seven categories listed here. For example, the gift of hospitality could fall under the headings of either mercy or service. The gift of encouragement might be under the category of exhortation.

Remember, this is not a scientific test with absolute answers. But it does give you a good starting point for considering what your spiritual gift(s) may be.

• • •

An Eye-Opener

Later in this book, I'll say more about how a teen's spiritual gifts can fit into his dreams for vocation and service. For now, the discovery process itself offers two fantastic benefits for both you and your teen.

First, it's one of the greatest "treasure hunts" you could ever embark upon with your adolescent. Second, it lets you steer your teen toward experiences that reveal and cultivate gifts that can be used for a lifetime.

》 "My mama would often speak of my strengths, and listening to pastors and teachers describe characteristics of certain gifts helped me to determine my gifts."
—*Heather W.*

Many Christian teens today are purposeless, their dreams foggy or nonexistent. That's partly because they don't know their spiritual gifts and how to exercise them.

Your young person doesn't have to be part of that trend. Lack of direction leads to trouble, but success leads to service. And service leads to the heart of God.

// WITH YOUR TEENAGER

Over a hot deep dish at your favorite pizza parlor, try the following:

- If she hasn't already done so, have her take the spiritual gifts inventory in this chapter. Work through another copy of the inventory yourself, with your teen's gifts in mind.
- Compare the two sets of answers. Are they in the same ballpark? If not, look at differences. Do you see gifts in your teen that she hasn't noticed? Do you feel strongly about some things on the lists, but you haven't told your teen?
- Ask: "If we've identified a gift you seem to have, how might you start putting that to use? Let's brainstorm some projects you could try that would test what we learned from this inventory."

6

identifying your teen's brain preference

When asked about his brain preference, Arthur simply answered, "Yes."

Another part of your teen's uniqueness is his or her brain preference—brain *hemisphere* preference, to be exact.

What do I mean by that? Well, I'm no psychologist. Fortunately, Focus on the Family's Tim Sanford is a licensed, professional counselor. I'm indebted to him for many of the fascinating brain facts that follow—as well as the self-test designed to help your teen determine his or her brain preference. Be sure to read the following introduction to the self-test, a version of which appears in the CD-ROM guide for teens, to discover what this aspect of your child's wiring means—and why it's so important.

• • •

EXPLORING YOUR BRAIN PREFERENCE

Your brain has two separate but connected halves known as the left and right hemispheres. Each controls different ways of thinking and perceiving. You use both sides of your brain, but you have a preference for one over the other.

Which side is better? Neither. Some people use one side or the other almost exclusively; some use mostly one side and a little of the other; some use each side almost equally. But for all of us, one side still functions more easily and naturally.

When you do something that's in line with your brain preference, it doesn't take a huge effort. But a task that requires using the other side of your brain makes it work 50 to 100 percent harder.

The left side of your brain handles sequential, logical, rational thought. Memorizing, spelling, vocabulary, language, and mathematical formulas come easily to it. So do following rules and making decisions based on logic, proof, and facts.

The left side deals with the world the way it is—its reality and rules. That hemisphere helps you adjust to fit your environment. If there are no rules for a specific situation, the left side will make some up.

The right side of your brain, meanwhile, is in charge of creativity and feelings. While the left side takes bits of information and arranges them in a logical order, the right side entertains random thought patterns.

Learning things that require sequences or memorizing—like spelling, vocabulary, language, and mathematical formulas—makes the right-brained person cringe. Memorizing Bible verses "word perfectly" is hard for the right brain because it understands the general idea but has difficulty grasping the details. Following directions is often a problem for the right side as it skims over instructions, gets the basic idea, and leaps ahead without reading the fine print.

Right-brain thinking wants to see or feel the real object—not symbols like words, letters, and mathematical notations. It follows its intuition. Instead of dealing with the world as it is, the right side looks for the way things could be. It asks, "Can the rules be changed?"

What does all this mean for your future? It means you'd better take your brain preference into account as you consider the kind of work you'll do and where you'll do it. If you're left-brained, for instance, you might not mind an office where all employees are required to leave their window blinds at exactly half-mast every night. If you're right-brained, you might prefer a company where employees have to crawl through a hole in the wall to get to a "conference room" that has pillows covering the floor.

Whether you're at work or in school, your brain will want to stay on the side where it functions most naturally. Forcing yourself to use the "other" side of your brain *all* the time can lead to headaches, fatigue, burnout, and frequent illnesses—not to mention procrastination, frustration, mistakes, poor concentration, moodiness, memory problems, and a pretty low view of yourself. As you dream about your future, remember that some experts recommend trying to spend at least 70 percent of your waking time operating from "your" hemisphere. It's a goal worth thinking about—in your own way, of course.

So what's your brain hemisphere preference? Here's another test from Focus on the Family counselor Tim Sanford, who provided many of the preceding insights on the brain. The test is divided into two sections. Each is different, so read the directions carefully.

SECTION ONE

Below are two lists of statements. Read over each and mark every statement that you think describes you at least 51 percent of the time (not the ones you would *like* to describe you). If you're not sure about a statement, leave it blank and come back to it later if you want. When you're done, add up the number of statements you marked on each list, and put the total at the bottom.

LIST ONE

___ When I read a novel, I read every word to get all the details.

___ I like to have things in sequence and in order.

___ I work well within an established structure.

___ I count on information more than intuition.

___ I like team sports more than individual ones.

___ I tend to be deliberate, conservative, and logical when spending money.

___ I can be very competitive, and I like to win.

___ I can make good decisions, even under pressure.

___ Algebra is easier to understand than geometry.

___ When I'm with my friends, I tend to take charge.

___ It's easy for me to remember people's names.

___ I like to know the rules and stick to them.

___ In math class, I can explain how I got the answer.

___ I tend to be neat and organized.

___ I want to motivate others.

___ I'm not very musical or artistic.

___ On tests, I prefer objective questions (true/false, multiple choice, matching) over essay questions.

___ I'm not very emotional.

___ I like making lists of things I have to do and marking them off when they're completed.

___ I have and like using a daily planner.

___ I can organize people to reach a common goal.

___ I'm good at paying attention to details.

___ Spelling is not that hard for me.

___ I follow directions easily.

___ People see me as a logical, organized person.

___ Memorizing phone numbers, vocabulary words, and math formulas seems easy.

___ I tend to set goals and achieve them.

___ When others tell me "no," I usually accept it.

___ I tend to analyze things a lot.

___ I'd rather express myself by talking than by drawing.

___ I seem to have a good memory.

____ **Total number of statements marked on this list**

LIST TWO

___ Remembering faces is a lot easier than remembering names.

___ I have a hard time recalling and/or following directions.

___ I often have hunches and follow them.

___ My room tends to be cluttered.

___ When I read a novel, I usually skip the details so I can get the main idea.

___ Geometry is easier to understand than algebra.

___ Spelling and grammar are hard for me to grasp.

___ I count on intuition more than information.

___ Routine is boring.

___ I can be impulsive, extravagant, and spontaneous when it comes to spending money.

___ I like high-risk activities.

___ When I'm on vacation, I don't want to be locked into a schedule.

___ I collect souvenirs and memorabilia.

___ When speaking, I often use lots of hand gestures.

___ In math class I can get the right answer, but I can't always show how I got it.

___ Having to use a daily planner would cramp my style, and it wouldn't help anyway.

___ On tests, I prefer essay or discussion questions to objective ones.

___ I'm often told I'm creative and imaginative but don't put out enough effort.

___ I want to see the whole picture.

___ I tend to base decisions more on how I feel than on how I think.

___ I like to nurture and encourage others.

___ I tend to take lots of chances.

___ I work better at my own pace and on my own time.

___ I try to pull people together so they can work well together.

___ I want to know why.

___ I often spend time thinking of ways around the rules.

___ I tend to daydream.

___ I can get the basic idea of something, but I can't seem to memorize very well.

___ When people tell me "no," I usually think, Well, why not?

___ I'm artistic or musical.

___ Colors seem to fascinate me.

_____ Total number of statements marked on this list

SECTION TWO

Below are 15 pairs of words and phrases. Some of these are opposites; some are not. Read both in each set and circle the one that describes you at least 51 percent of the time. When you're done, add up the number of words circled in each column and put the total at the bottom.

logical	dreamer
thinker	senser
goal setter	idea generator
fan of stability	fan of change
routine	different
problem solver	brainstormer
grounded in reality	soaring in imagination

task completer	relationship mender
prioritizer	visualizer
organizer	harmonizer
systematic	emotional
traditional	unconventional
maintainer	connecter
detail person	global viewer
rule respecter	freedom fighter

_____ Total number of words   _____ Total number of words
     or phrases circled   or phrases circled

And now, let's analyze the results of your brain exam.

If list one has more check marks than list two, and more items are circled in the first column of section two than in the second column, you're probably a "lefty" when it comes to brain preference.

As you think about what classes to take in the future, remember that subjects like these may be easier for you and other left-brained people:

Math (algebra, statistics, or calculus)

History, civics

Reading

Technical writing

Research

Electrical engineering

Public speaking, debate team

Typing

Accounting, bookkeeping

How about jobs? You may do best with positions that allow you to set goals and make decisions, that call on you to improve what already exists, that ask you to prioritize, analyze, maintain routine, and pay attention to details.

In which career fields do you find more left-brained people?

Corporate presidents, chief financial officers

Lawyers

Physicians

Accountants, bookkeepers, auditors

Dentists

Electrical and electronic engineers

Assembly-line workers

Managers and supervisors of all types

Operating room and intensive care nurses

Mechanics or machinists

On the other hand—or hemisphere—you're probably more right-brained if list two has more checks than list one and if you circled more items in the second column under section two.

Which subjects in school may be easier for right-brained people?

Math (geometry, trigonometry)

Biology

Music

Creative writing

Foreign languages

Drama, dance, choreography

Chemistry, physics

Art, design

Philosophy, sociology, cultural anthropology

As for jobs, consider those that allow you to see the big picture and brainstorm in order to find solutions to problems. You'll probably do best with opportunities that let you create new products or ideas, encourage other people, and allow your artistic bent to show.

In which career fields do you find more right-brained people?

Consultants of all types

Philosophers

Emergency room physicians, psychiatrists

Artists, writers, entertainers, musicians, composers

Elementary and high school teachers and coaches

Actors, dancers

Designers, interior decorators

Counselors, chaplains

Public relations, marketing
Pediatricians, pediatric nurses

Now, go back and circle any careers listed in this section that appeal to you. Then come up with two more that you think might fit your brain preference.

• • •

A Warning to Parents

When it comes to brain hemisphere preference, there's a danger we parents need to watch out for: long-term adaptation.

That phrase may not sound too scary, but its meaning is. It's estimated that, due to social expectations and pressures, about 70 percent of teens try to make themselves work on the "wrong" side of their brains.

Why? For one thing, our education system largely caters to the functions of the left side of the brain. Left-brained students tend to excel in school and reap the recognition that comes with such achievement.

Extremely right-brained students may be wrongly labeled as lazy, underachieving, uncooperative, or having Attention Deficit Hyperactivity Disorder (ADHD). They can be misdiagnosed as having learning disabilities, especially in language and reading. Right-brained students may also have a harder time taking tests and meeting deadlines. Right-brained students, especially boys, are more likely to drop out of school; right-brained teens account for the vast majority of patients in adolescent psychiatric units of hospitals.

>> "My parents supported me and most of my dreams. They always encouraged me and believed that I was a smart person despite what my teachers said."

—Joel

Gender expectations also lead right-brained kids to try forcing themselves to be left-brained. Boys, pressed to exhibit "masculine" left-brained traits like leadership, decision-making, being a team player, and thinking logically and sequentially, attempt to suppress "feminine" right-brained tendencies toward fluid body movement, art, imaginative thinking, question asking, and solitude. Our teen boys need to know they can be very male *and* right-brained.

Right-brained females, on the other hand, may be mislabeled as weak, timid, or "overly emotional" just because they're tenderhearted and more likely to express their feelings. They may be pressured to act "more logical," be tougher, and go toe-to-toe with males.

Left-brained females can suffer too—especially if they're strongly extroverted. Often they find themselves called "mannish" or "bossy" and a host of other disrespectful words. Our girls need to know that it's possible to be feminine and left-brained—as well as right-brained and strong.

Right-brained teens adapt away from their brain preference more often than their left-brained counterparts. If your teen's test results are nearly the same for both sides, some level of adaptation may be present.

Adapting away from our natural brain preference over a long period can cause physical harm. At first it just requires more mental energy. But after a while, it may cause headaches, fatigue, procrastination, frustration, an unusually high number of random errors, poor concentration, moodiness, memory problems, poor self-esteem, feelings of incompetence, and even damage to the autoimmune system. Of course, these symptoms can originate from other sources, physical or psychological. If you see some of these signs in your teen, seek a medical examination and a more in-depth brain preference assessment before coming to any firm conclusions.

In the next chapter we'll look at a part of your teen's wiring that may be a little more familiar—the part that tends to make him an extrovert or an introvert.

// WITH YOUR TEENAGER

Over a tall glass of iced tea or a mug of hot chocolate (depending on the season), try the following:

- If your teen hasn't already done so, have him take the brain preference assessment included in this chapter. Work through another copy of the test yourself, with your teen in mind.
- Compare the two sets of answers. Did you come up with similar results? If not, look at differences. Do you see traits in your teen that she hasn't noticed?
- Review together the symptoms of trying to adapt away from one's natural brain preference. Then ask: "Do you think you've been trying to adapt away from your preference? If so, is the pressure to do that coming from me, from school, or from some other source? What can we do to change that?"

7

discovering whether your teen is an extrovert or introvert

*As an extrovert, Rikki found her summer job
as a lighthouse keeper slightly less than ideal.*

Having authored a few books in my time, I've noticed that there are two kinds of editors. The first wants to take a manuscript, go off in a quiet corner alone, and fix the text without interruption. The second likes to go out and brainstorm with authors (or at least talk with them on the phone), chat with co-workers, and spend as little time as possible figuring out where all the commas should go.

Both kinds can get the job done. But ask one from the first group to work like the second—or vice versa—and the results can be painful for all concerned.

That was Ted's experience.

As a boy, Ted loved to curl up with a good story. In his imagination he could travel the world, even to other worlds like C. S. Lewis's Narnia. His fondness for books made him want a career working with the written word.

After college, Ted found a job as a book editor. He loved to polish sentences and bring order to the most confused paragraph, and he was good at it.

Definitely in the first group of editors, Ted would go into his "cocoon" of an office at the start of the day and rarely be seen again until quitting time. His perfect day was one without a phone call or other interruption. As far as he was concerned, authors were a necessary but annoying part of the process.

One day his boss decided to reward Ted's performance by giving him a promotion. The change would mean working much more closely with authors; the boss said it would be more creative and fulfilling. Ted was reluctant, being perfectly content with what he was doing, but the bigger paycheck was persuasive.

By the end of his third project in the new position, Ted was miserable. Much of his time was now spent in meetings and on the phone. Instead of polishing sentences himself, he was trying to get authors to do it themselves. His work had gone from joy to burden, from source of satisfaction to endless headache.

After toughing it out for a year, Ted turned in his resignation—and went looking for a new job like his old one.

Why were Ted and his new job such a mismatch? Because he was an introvert, and his position called for the opposite. As you may have figured, people in the first group I described tend to be introverts; those in the second are usually extroverts.

But what do those terms really mean? It's important to find out, and to find out where your teen falls on the extrovert/introvert continuum. It's a part of his wiring that may determine whether today's dreams of career and service become tomorrow's nightmares.

The following self-test, provided by Focus on the Family counselor Tim Sanford, will help you and your teen better understand this aspect of his or her uniqueness. Be sure to read the test yourself, a version of which appears in the CD-ROM guide for teens. You'll find out a lot about what it means to be an introvert or extrovert and how it can affect your young person's future.

●　●　●　————————————————————————————————

ARE YOU AN INNIE OR AN OUTIE?

Extroverts are outies. They tend to put their "best foot forward"; the strengths of their personalities are aimed outward to interact with the world. With an extrovert, what you see is who he is—like an open book.

Introverts are innies. Instead of putting their "best foot" forward, they tend to reserve the strongest part of their personalities and keep it focused inward, out of the world's view. With an introvert, what you see is just the shell—like an oyster.

People can be "innies" or "outies" to varying degrees; you don't have to be totally one or the other. But it's good to know your tendency as you dream about the future.

Being extroverted or introverted isn't a matter of whether you "like people" or "don't like people." It's about where you go to get energy and where you focus most of your concentration. Introverts find energy in their inner world of ideas, so they require less from the outside world. Extroverts find their energy in things and people; pulled by this outer life of action and interaction, they spend less time with thoughts and concepts.

Can you have both "innie" and "outie" traits? Sure. It's like being a switch-hitter in baseball. A good switch-hitter can hit the ball well either right- or left-handed. His batting average may even be close to the same from both sides. But one way is still naturally easier for him. In the same way, a good basketball player can shoot a layup with either hand, yet one is naturally easier. That's what your preference is: what's naturally easier for you.

Is it better to be an innie or an outie? Neither. As with the other aspects of your makeup, both preferences have their strengths. Both have their shortcomings, too.

Not everybody understands this, though. Our society tends to accept extroverts more easily than it does introverts. This is especially true for introverted teen guys, who are often seen as loners, social misfits, or depressed. They may try to force themselves to act like extroverts so that people will see them as go-getter, take-charge types. If that's happening to you, think about the stress it's causing you—and will cause in the future if you keep it up. Look for friends who will accept you as you are; ask a parent, pastor, or counselor for help if your efforts to be someone you're not are causing you trouble.

Here's an assessment tool, compliments of counselor Tim Sanford, that can help you better understand where you fall on the extrovert-introvert scale. Remember that you're just trying to get a general idea of your preference—not trying to fit yourself in a tight little box.

Read the two lists of statements below. Mark every statement that you think describes you at least 51 percent of the time (not the ones you would *like* to have describe you). If you're not sure about one, leave it blank and come back to it later if you want.

LIST ONE

___ I'd rather watch others at a party than be the center of attention.

___ I want to understand the things around me.

___ I often keep my feelings to myself.

___ Being with people (even if I like them) tires me out after a while.

___ I think I understand myself fairly well.

___ When I say, "I've been thinking about . . ." it means I've been thinking about something for a long time and have it figured out enough to share it with you.

___ To communicate, I'd rather write than talk.

___ I have a few deep friendships.

___ People see me as reserved or detached.

___ I tend to be more calm than energetic.

___ I tend to be quiet.

___ I enjoy spending time alone.

___ People have to spend time with me before they know who I am.

___ When I'm in a group, I prefer talking to one person at a time.

___ It's easier for me to be introduced than to introduce myself.

___ I often feel I'm the last to know what's going on with my group of friends.

___ I feel comfortable talking at length to people only after I get to know them.

___ I don't seem as enthusiastic about things as other people do.

_____ **Total number of statements marked**

LIST TWO

___ It's easy for me to mingle at a party.

___ New people can tell what I'm interested in right away.

___ I show my feelings freely.

___ People say I'm easy to get to know.

___ It's important for me to always know what's going on around me.

___ I have a lot of friendships.

___ I'm a talkative person.

___ To communicate, I'd rather talk than write.

___ I like to be where the "action" is.

___ I freely share my thoughts and opinions.

___ Being with lots of people energizes and motivates me.

___ In a crowd, it's easy for me to introduce myself and others.

___ I always seem to know what's going on with my group of friends.

___ I want to be a catalyst for change.

___ When I say, "I've been thinking about . . ." it means I just now had the thought and I want to share it with you.

___ It's easy for me to get to know other people.

___ I'm up on all the latest fashions.

___ I feel energized after a party.

_____ **Total number of statements marked**

So, are you an innie? Let's find outie.

If you made more checks on list two than on list one, you're probably more of an extrovert. You tend to like action and get along well in social settings. You're likely to be an optimist. You get bored or impatient with slow jobs and slow people, enjoy talking on the phone, and are generally confident and relaxed. You tend to work well under pressure, like when you take tests. Your slogan may be, "What's next?"

What jobs do extroverts tend to like? Look for those that provide lots of activity, variety, and stimulating input. You'll probably do best where you have plenty of interaction with people, many things going on at the same time, and deadlines to meet. Extroverts also enjoy jobs that let them turn ideas into reality.

In which career fields do we find more-extroverted people? Here are some:

Marketing

Restaurant managers and workers

Actors

Salespeople and sales managers

Dental hygienists

Bank and office managers

Religious and personal service workers

Hairdressers and cosmetologists

Self-employed business people

Teachers

And what if your list one has more checks than list two? Then you're probably more introverted. You tend to focus your energies inward; you're energized by times when you can be alone to ponder your thoughts, let your mind wander. You need time to reflect before taking action. You're always asking questions (though not always out loud), tend to be more negative than positive in your outlook, and may get tagged as a pessimist. If you like sports, it's probably the more solitary ones. You can work contentedly by yourself on a job, and you probably prefer sending E-mail and notes instead of talking directly to a person. You tend not to work so well under the pressure of exams. Your slogan may be, "I wonder why . . . ?"

What kinds of jobs work well for introverts? Consider those that allow you to work alone for much of the time, and where the stimulation level is low. You'll probably do best where you can have your own quiet space and work at your own pace. You may prefer an environment with fewer deadlines, one that lets you think up ideas and overcome the challenges that stand in the way of their becoming reality.

In which career fields do we find more-introverted people?

Electrical and electronic engineers

Chemists and other scientists

Librarians, archivists, and curators

Mechanics and other repair people

Lawyers

Computer programmers

Physicians

Health technicians

Priests and monks

College professors

While you shouldn't pick a career based only on whether you're extroverted or introverted, where you land on the scale will affect your work performance—and satisfaction.

• • •

Another Warning to Parents

Chances are that you won't be completely surprised by your teen's test results. You know whether she likes being part of the action, whether she gets along well in social settings, whether she likes to meet new people and talk with them. You know how much time she spends on the phone, whether she often fails to think before speaking, and how well she works under pressure.

You might not realize, however, that your teen's wiring in this area can cause problems—especially if he or she is in the introverted minority.

Extroverted people are more easily understood and accepted by our society. This is especially true for males; introverted teen boys are often seen as timid at best and "dangerous loners" at worst. The pressure for introverts to act like extroverts is enormous.

If God has wired your teen to be an introvert, are you willing to accept that? Or are you tempted to push your young person toward the other end of the scale, fearing he'll never be a success if he doesn't "come out of his shell"?

On the other hand, if your teen is an extrovert and you're not, can you accept it—even if her "social butterfly routine" tends to wear you out?

True, it's sometimes necessary to nudge our teens out of their comfort zones in order to help them grow. But if your child's scores on the preceding assessment are equal or within one or two points of being equal, consider that she may be squelching her natural tendencies in order to please family or friends. Some people are equally

›› "My mom traded in the piano for my guitar. She believed in me!"
—*Jacob*

extroverted and introverted, but it's more likely that adapting is taking place.

In a world made by such a creative Creator, it really does take all kinds—"innies" and "outies." Finding out what kind your teen is, and helping him make the most of it, will go a long way toward realizing those God-honoring dreams.

// WITH YOUR TEENAGER

Over sundaes at your local ice cream shop, try the following:

- If your teen hasn't already done so, have him complete the self-assessment in this chapter. Work through another copy yourself, with your teen in mind. Also take the test to find your own position on the extrovert/introvert continuum.

- Compare the three assessments. Do you and your teen agree on where the two of you fall on the continuum? Ask, "If these results are correct, what does it say about how you and I can relate to each other better?"

- Ask, "Do you ever feel pressured by me to try to be something you're not in this area? What could we use as a secret signal or code word between us so that you can alert me when you're feeling that way?"

pinpointing your teen's sensory preference

Despite learning that he was visually oriented, young Michelangelo was determined to become a concert harmonica player.

Danielle struggled mightily to follow her teachers' lectures. She would listen intently, take copious notes, and strain her brain to understand what was being taught. Yet after just two or three minutes of a lesson, she'd be lost and in despair.

The same thing would happen when her softball coach explained how a play was supposed to work. Danielle just couldn't follow the verbal instruction.

But when a teacher or coach would write or draw things on a chalk-board—a math problem, say, or the steps to be followed in a science experiment, or the movement of the ball on an infield play—Danielle understood and applied the lesson immediately.

Danielle's experience was all about *sensory preference*. Her teachers and coaches were used to giving instruction through *hearing*, while Danielle was wired for *visual* processing.

Your teen has sensory preferences, too. To find out more about the concept and its implications for your teen's dreams, read the following section. It includes information from Dr. Arlene Taylor and counselor Tim Sanford. Dr. Taylor's "Sensory Preference Assessment" also appears in the companion guide for teens on the CD-ROM.

• • • ————————————————————————————

FINDING YOUR SENSORY PREFERENCE

Human beings relate to the world and each other using the senses. Experts have defined three sensory systems through which people tend to "take in" the world: visual (seeing), auditory (hearing), and kinesthetic (touch, taste, smell). You have a sensory preference, too. It has a big influence on whether you're succeeding or struggling in school—and on the kind of career that may fit you in the future.

Your sensory preference refers to the type of sensory input that registers *most quickly* in your brain. Unimpaired, we are able to use *all* the senses. But each of us tends to rely on sight, sound, or touch for more of our "data collecting" than on our other senses. We feel most comfortable and understood when we get data through our preferred system—visual, auditory, or kinesthetic.

Which of the three senses is best? None. All have their place. We may be aware of one over the other two depending on the environment. For example, we may be more aware of touch while petting the cat, more aware of sound when listening to music, and more aware of vision while watching TV. We can become *competent* in any of the three senses—but we still have a *natural preference* for one.

Collecting information through your preferred system comes easily and energy efficiently. That's why you tend to gravitate toward, and return to, environments that reward your sensory preference.

Take Christopher, for instance. His preference is visual. If you saw his room, you'd understand; the walls are plastered with posters of his favorite Japanese anime characters. Not surprisingly, he loves to go to the mall and window shop—just soaking up the sights. He spends a lot of time drawing pictures on his computer, and he hopes to be a video game designer someday.

His twin brother Jonathan, on the other hand, has a strong streak of "kinesthetic" in him. For him, touch is important. He wore soft sweat pants until he was 12 because jeans felt too scratchy. When he comes home from school, he picks up the cat and rubs his cheek on her fur. He likes to play basketball, and he thinks he might try to be a sportswriter after college.

Being visual doesn't mean you need to become a photographer; being auditory doesn't mean you should be a professional musician; being kinesthetic doesn't mean you must throw footballs or potter's clay for a living. But knowing what type of sensory stimuli gets your attention most quickly can help you focus on activities and situations that match your preference. It can also help you to understand why you feel more comfortable in some environments and less comfortable in others.

Here's a tool that can help you to think about the senses in a new way and identify your own sensory preference.[1] Read each statement. If it applies to you *at least 75 percent of the time,* mark the line in front of it. Otherwise, leave the line blank and move on to the next statement.

LIST ONE

___ I learn a lot about people from the sound and/or tone of their voices.

___ Sounds usually catch my attention quickly.

___ I talk to myself frequently, aloud, under my breath, and/or in whispers.

___ I keep up with current events by listening to radio news more than by watching television.

___ I would rather listen to an audiocassette or CD than read a book.

___ Others consider me chatty or sometimes say that I talk too much.

___ I tend to "hear" the voice of the author when reading a personal E-mail or letter.

___ Strange noises, rattles, or repetitive sounds in my vehicle or house annoy/worry me.

___ I talk to my pets as I would to close friends.

___ I use rhyming words to help me remember names, labels, dates, or other facts.

___ Jingles and acronyms help me to recall information.

___ I study for exams by verbalizing my notes and/or key points aloud.

___ I repeat new words to myself to help fix them in memory.

___ I enjoy humming, whistling, or singing (alone or in a group).

___ I especially appreciate musical programs or concerts.

___ Talk shows and interview programs appeal to me.

___ I often enjoy verbal discussions including long telephone or ham-radio conversations.

___ I am usually considered an attentive listener.

___ I enjoy listening to audiocassettes, books on tape, records, and CDs.

___ I can't stand the sound of jangling keys or a dripping faucet.

___ I often use expressions such as "Sounds right," "I hear you," "Keep your ears open."

Auditory Score = _____ out of 21

LIST TWO

___ I like to control the lighting in my environment (e g., dimmer controls, spotlights, uplights, mood lighting).

___ I purchase items primarily based on looks/visual appeal.

___ I tend to select clothes because they look good/sharp.

___ I avoid wearing clothing that is mismatched in color, pattern, or design.

___ I like to keep my vehicle washed, waxed, and looking good.

___ I prefer a map to receiving verbal or printed directions.

___ When eating, the presentation of the food/table/environment is very important.

___ I learn a lot about people from their appearances.

___ I often see something before I hear, sense, or feel it.

___ I rarely bump into or stumble over objects that I didn't see.

___ I prefer to see people when communicating with them.

___ When shopping, I want the products to be clearly and attractively displayed.

___ I prefer pets that I can watch (e.g., fish in a tank, birds).

___ I often say things like "The light just went on," "I see what you mean," "Looks okay to me."

___ A picture or diagram is worth a thousand words.

___ I prefer to watch TV/movies/videos as compared to reading the book or a script.

___ I prefer books/magazines that contain graphs, pictures, or colorful illustrations.

___ I really enjoy looking at photo albums.

___ It's important that my living/work spaces look visually attractive.

___ Mirrors are important fixtures in my home.

___ When selecting a place to live, the view from my abode is of major concern.

Visual Score = _____ out of 21

LIST THREE

___ I'm very sensitive to odor, taste, temperature, and texture.

___ I can usually recognize objects quite easily by touch in the dark.

___ I tend to select clothes because they feel good and are comfortable to wear.

___ If purchasing a vehicle, room and comfort are very important considerations.

___ I prefer frequent changes in body position and move often.

___ I often use expressions such as "My sense is," "That fits," "I've got a handle on it."

___ I enjoy getting physical exercise (e.g., walking, hiking, cycling, jogging).

___ I like to work out and/or take jazzercise or yoga classes.

___ I'd rather participate in sports than observe others playing.

___ I enjoy soaking in the tub or basking in the warm sunshine.

___ I like to receive and/or give back rubs and massages.

___ I enjoy touching and hugging my friends.

___ I readily learned the touch method for keyboards and/or data entry systems.

___ I have good physical coordination.

___ I learn a lot about people from their handshakes, hugs, or touch.

___ I often tap my toes or feel like moving my body (e.g., dancing) to music/a beat.

___ I like to hold babies or pets that I can touch, stroke, and cuddle.

___ I especially enjoy making things with my hands (e.g., carving, sculpture, woodwork, crocheting, knitting, sewing, finger painting, various crafts).

___ I prefer being outdoors over indoors whenever possible.

___ Above all, my furniture must be comfortable.

___ I prefer my home and vehicles to be climate controlled for comfort.

Kinesthetic Score = _____ out of 21

Now take a look at your scores on the three lists.

The list with the highest total score likely represents your overall sensory preference. If two scores are tied, one may represent your preference and the other a sensory system you've had to develop in order to relate to people and things in your environment. If one of those tied scores is kinesthesia, it's possible that your natural preference is kinesthetic and you've pulled back from it. If all your scores are equal, that's not a naturally occurring pattern. Use this clue to evaluate relationships in your family. Could you be stifling your natural sensory preference and developing one that's more "acceptable" at home?

Auditory people tend to prefer careers that let them use their ability to listen and talk. In which fields do we find them? Here are some examples:

Musicians, singers, and instrumentalists

Psychotherapists, counselors

Speech therapists

Talk-show hosts

Public speakers

Radio broadcasters

Telephone communicators

Foreign language translators

Visual people tend to gravitate toward careers that allow them to use their sensitivity to appearance—both in absorbing information and in expressing themselves. They usually excel at tasks that require "eagle eyes."

In which career fields do we find visual people? Here are some examples:

Airline pilots

Firefighters

Sharpshooters, marksmen

TV or movie entertainers

Designers

Models

Sign-language translators

Air traffic controllers

Kinesthetic people tend to select careers that allow them to express themselves in physical ways and in tasks that require "the right touch."

In which career fields do we find kinesthetic people? Here are examples:

Athletes

Dancers

Surgeons

Physical, occupational, or massage therapists

Computer programmers
Artists (painting, pottery, sculpting)
Sign-language translators
Mechanics, machinists
Chefs, cooks

• • •

Do You Recognize Your Teen?

In addition to using the assessment, you can help to identify your teen's sensory preference by observing her and recalling what she was like as a youngster. Here are some things to look for—and remember.

Auditory people tend to exhale deeply and sigh, especially when they're tired, tense, or stressed. They may cock their heads to one side in order to hear better, sometimes even cupping or touching their ears in the process. As children, they preferred pets and toys that made interesting sounds. They may have been prone to fear loud or scary noises such as storms, sirens, or crying people. Their food has to "sound right"; they may not like the sound of crunchy foods, or they may feel that crunchy cereal has to "crunch" or it won't taste right. The sounds of clothing are important to them; swishing fabrics and clanking zippers may either bother or comfort them. They're likely to be hurt by harsh words or voice tones, a lack of soothing verbal affirmation, or being given the silent treatment.

>> "Both of my parents had me take a 'test for success,' an aptitude test, around my freshman or sophomore year in high school. That really showed me what my strengths were, how I best study, and what occupations would satisfy my needs and personality."
>> —*Heather A.*

Visual people tend to draw pictures in the air with their hands and arms. They're likely to speak rapidly and may have a higher pitch to their voices. As children, they preferred pets that were interesting to watch—

and colorful, attractive toys that moved. They may have been prone to fear of the dark or of scary shadows, movies, or pictures. Their food had to "look right"; their beets and mashed potatoes couldn't run together. Clothes must look right, too; many visual people can't imagine how anyone could wear outmoded styles. They like you to look at them during conversations, and may be hurt by lack of eye contact when talking with another person.

Kinesthetic people often prefer to work with their hands. They tend to speak more slowly and have lower-pitched voices. As children, they may have preferred pets that were comfortable to touch and may have been intuitive where animals were concerned. The texture of toys was important—smooth, soft, or otherwise interesting. They may have been prone to fear physical pain or discomfort. Their food had to "feel right, smell right, and taste right"—not too hot or cold, not slimy or jagged. Their clothes must fit comfortably, without restriction or irritation or scratchy tags that rub against the skin. Kinesthetic people can't imagine how anyone could wear uncomfortable clothes just because that's the style. They're sensitive to air temperature and the feel of furniture. They may be hurt by the lack of gentle touch or by harsh touch, such as rough horseplay or being held down or tickled.

Still Another Warning for Parents

If two of your teen's scores are tied on the assessment, one probably represents his preference—and the other a sensory system he's had to develop in order to relate to people and things in his environment. If one of those scores is kinesthetic, consider the strong possibility that your teen's natural preference is kinesthetic—and that he's pulled back from it for some reason. For example, has he not received sufficient affirming, physical, nonsexual touch? Or has he been touched roughly or painfully?

Most schools cater mainly to auditory, left-brained people. From middle school on, most teaching is done in lecture format—verbally given and auditorily received. Visual students often can compensate by studying handouts, graphs, and diagrams. But kinesthetic students, who are usually weakest in auditory perceiving, have a hard time with classroom lectures and homework. Kids who are kinesthetic *and* right-brained have it even harder.

If your teen is kinesthetic, he'll do best when material is presented in a hands-on, project-oriented way. He'll also be more likely to thrive if his greater need for touch is met through appropriate, nonsexual routes—like a hug or pat on the back from Dad or Mom.

If your teen has been shamed or injured because of his sensory preference, he may have adapted into a "safer" one. Since he uses all his senses anyway, this adaptation may work—but takes more energy and wears on his emotional and physical health.

All Together Now

Talk about wired! We've put your teen's circuitry under the microscope in the last few chapters, haven't we? We've explored his uniqueness as a person created by a loving God—personality, interests and passions, spiritual gifts, brain preference, extroversion or introversion, and sensory preference.

What can we do with all those puzzle pieces? In the next chapter, we'll start putting them together. It's time to look at the bigger picture of lifetime dreams that God may have prepared your teen to pursue.

// WITH YOUR TEENAGER

Over a Saturday breakfast at your favorite pancake place, try the following:
- If your teen hasn't already done so, have her take the sensory preference assessment included in this chapter. Take the assessment yourself to help identify your own sensory preference. Are your results similar or different? Are you nurturing and affirming your teen in his or her sensory preference?

- Compare your own sensory preference with your teen's. Describe how jobs you've held or interests you've pursued have—or haven't—fit your preference.
- Ask: "Now that we know more about your sensory preference, would it help to change anything about the way you study? If so, what?"

9

putting the puzzle together

With typical efficiency, Sandy combined her search for career guidance with her fondness for low-fat desserts.

Did your teen work through the self-tests in the preceding chapters? If so, do you think the results were accurate?

If you doubt those results, take a moment to think about what might be going on in your teen's life right now. Depression, stress, past trauma, anxiety, sin, rebellion, unhealthy family dynamics, excessive adapting in order to gain acceptance—any of these can distort those evaluations. If your teen is suffering in one or more of these areas, put the self-tests aside for a while and work on the problem. Don't hesitate to seek help from your youth pastor or a counselor if needed.

But if you and your teen agree that the exercises have produced some pretty good hints about the way he or she is wired, it's time to start pulling those hints together. The question is, how? Do all these labels and numbers point the way to fulfilling, God-honoring dreams—or are they just an explosion in a psychobabble factory?

It's a good thing our friend Tim Sanford has provided the following exercise. You'll want to read it carefully and work through it with your son or daughter. A version also appears in the companion guide for teens on CD-ROM.

● ● ● ———————————————————————————————————

PUTTING YOUR PUZZLE TOGETHER

Does your right (or left) brain hurt after taking all those assessments? Does finding out that you're an introvert make you want to crawl into a hole? Does your kinesthetic sensory preference have you grabbing this guide and trying to break it in half?

It's time to quit taking tests for a while and do something with what you've learned about your wiring. But how can you pull it all together? How can all those exams point the way to possible dreams that could fulfill you and honor God?

The following activity from counselor Tim Sanford will help.

1. Look back at your extroverted/introverted assessment (chapter 7). Highlight the descriptions that seem to fit you best.

2. Turn to the tool that looked at your left/right brain preference (chapter 6). Highlight the descriptions there that really seem to fit you.

3. Put your extroverted/introverted and your left/right brain preference tests together, and find the things you've highlighted on both. Which traits are repeated?

4. Look at the career suggestions included in both assessments; which ones are repeated?

5. Look at your sensory preference worksheet (chapter 8). What career fields are recommended there? Were any mentioned on the other tests?

Comparing these three tools is a good way to start sorting out career options. If several careers keep popping up, think about getting practical experience in each of those areas to find out which you like and dislike. If no strong themes emerge, consider retaking the assessments in about four weeks.

6. Now look at your Vision Quest (chapter 4). Do the patterns on your worksheet back up your findings on career options?

If not, why might that be? Have you not had the chance to let your strengths shine, or could there be another reason?

7. Lastly, look over your spiritual gifts inventory (chapter 5). While spiritual gifts aren't always employment-oriented, sometimes they are. How might your spiritual gifts work in the career fields you're considering?

Could your spiritual gifts be exercised in your "spare" time? How?

When you think about careers, there's a lot to consider. That's why it's important to get as much information about yourself as you can and then see how it all fits together.

Experts say it's best to structure your life so that about 70 percent of your waking hours are spent in areas where your preferences naturally lie. Life is much more than your career, of course, but since a job takes up a large part of those waking hours—working and thinking about work—you'll be much happier if your career fits your preferences.

For example, left-brained Meghan will do better to choose management over design. Right-brained Hunter will be better off becoming a biology teacher instead of an English teacher. Extrovert Brandon probably will be glad he pursued sales and not computer programming (and vice versa for introvert Jodie).

Even within a career field, it's good to look for a niche that fits you best. For instance, pediatrics is normally better for a right-brained nurse, while the intensive care unit usually will be a better fit for a left-brained nurse.

If you choose a career that doesn't match your brain preference, you'll need to make up for it in other areas of your life. If right-brained Kevin's job requires him to manage, schedule, and make decisions, he'll want to allow plenty of time for walks in the park, journal writing, and singing on the church worship team. These activities will give relief from the brain strain he feels at work.

If you're *left-brained and extroverted,* look into careers that involve:

Negotiating

Leadership

Goal setting and decision making

Management

Mechanics, repair

If you're *right-brained and extroverted,* look into careers that involve:

Troubleshooting

Entrepreneuring—starting new ventures

Self-directed activity (consultant, small business owner)

Marketing, public relations

Teaching, counseling

If you're *left-brained and introverted,* look into careers that involve:

Researching

Diagnosing

Accounting, bookkeeping

Engineering

Following detailed instructions accurately

And if you're *right-brained and introverted,* look for careers that involve:

Computer programming

Acting, music, or composing

Guiding, counseling, or pastoral activities

Self-directed work situations (resource specialist or consulting)

Designing new things

"Okay," you may be saying. "I'm ready to start looking at careers, but what are my choices? How many kinds of jobs are there, anyway?"

Good question! When you add up all the occupations in the world—everything from aardvark hunter to zymologist—there's no telling what the total might be. One site on the World Wide Web lists 12,000 job descriptions. Another catalogs 23,000 careers—and says that about 100,000 can be found in the 2000 U.S. Census and other sources!

How can you sort out the possibilities? A good place to start is "o*net OnLine," the Occupational Information Network sponsored by the U.S. Department of Labor. The Internet address is http://online. onetcenter.org. You might also try Netscape's career site at http://channels.netscape.com/ns/careers. Click on "Career Finder" for tests that try to match your personality and interests with specific occupations.

If you'd rather look in a book, ask your local reference librarian to show you the U.S. Department of Labor's Dictionary of Occupational Titles.

Don't discount any career option yet. Be open and willing to look at any field, even if you don't think you could do it or would like it right now.

Here are three Bible-based steps Tim Sanford recommends when you're trying to piece together your personal puzzle:

1. Observe and become aware of who you are. Psalm 139:14 says, "I praise you because I am fearfully and wonderfully made." Do you really believe God values you and has created you with unique abilities? Why or why not?

2. Evaluate yourself honestly. Psalm 139:23-24 says, "Search me, O God, and know my heart; test me and know my anxious thoughts. See if there is any offensive way in me, and lead me in the way everlasting." Have you asked God to show you your weaknesses as well as your strengths? If not, will you do that now?

3. Get honest feedback from others. According to Proverbs 11:14, "In the multitude of counselors there is safety" (KJV). How many "counselors" (parents, friends, pastors, teachers, etc.) have you asked for help in figuring out your future? Are you open to hearing things from them that make you a little uncomfortable? Or do you listen only to people who agree with you?

Following these three steps will help you develop mentally, physically, socially, and spiritually (see Luke 2:52) into the person God has designed you to become.

• • •

For More Information

Want to find out more about your teen's wiring? Here are just a few of the resources available:

- *Thriving in Mind,* by Katherine Benziger, Ph.D. (KBA Publications, 2000)
- *Myers-Briggs Type Indicator,* by Isabel Briggs Myers (available online or through a counselor)
- *Gifts Differing: Understanding Personality Type,* by Isabel Briggs Myers with Peter Myers (Davies-Black Publishing, 1995)
- *Please Understand Me: Character and Temperament Types,* by David Keirsey & Marilyn Bates (Prometheus Nemesis Book Co., 1984)
- *Type Talk,* by Otto Kroeger and Janet M. Thuesen (Delta, 1989)

- For a tool that helps one to identify personal brain preference, the *Benziger Thinking Styles Assessment* (BTSA), contact Arlene Taylor, Ph.D., Realizations Inc., P.O. Box 2554, Napa, CA 94558-0255. Ph: 707-554-4981, www.arlenetaylor.org.

// WITH YOUR TEENAGER

Over steaming cups at your local java joint, try the following:

- If your teen hasn't already done so, have him do the exercise in this chapter.
- Discuss the results. Do any possible careers or avocations stand out? If so, how does he feel about them? If not, does he need to retake the self-assessments in a little while or get more input from you and others who know him well?
- Ask: "In light of what we've learned so far, what's the biggest, most exciting dream you can imagine pursuing for the rest of your life? What can we do now to help you learn more about it or start taking steps in that direction?"

part three

finding your teen's place in the world

unleashing the power of mentors

*Roberto was beginning to doubt that his internship with Captain Ahab
would lead to a career in commercial fishing after all.*

Glenn Leatherwood must have been something special.

Most adults would have considered it sacrifice enough to teach a
Sunday school class of seventh-grade boys. But Glenn didn't stop there.
He took a genuine interest in the futures of four boys in that class. He
sensed potential in them, even believed that God might want them to go
into pastoral ministry.

Glenn had always been a good teacher, pouring love and God's Word
into all his students. But he made a concerted effort with those four boys,

encouraging them to think and pray and explore the possibility of becoming pastors. After planting that dream in their minds, he laid his hands on their heads and prayed for them.

All four of those boys went on to serve God as ministers. One of them was John Maxwell, now a noted author and speaker. He was just 13 when Glenn sparked that dream, but the experience shaped his life.

Says Maxwell today, "Although I wasn't officially ordained until about 10 years later, I've always considered Glenn Leatherwood's prayer for me that morning to be my official ordination into the ministry. . . . I consider Glenn Leatherwood to be one of the major influencers in my youth. He not only encouraged me to be a pastor, but he also ministered to me with his kindness and affection during the difficult junior-high years. He made an impact on me in a way my parents couldn't."[1]

In a word, Glenn Leatherwood was a mentor.

Another teen dreamed not of the pastorate but of practicing law. His imagination fueled by TV shows like *Perry Mason,* he thought he'd enjoy the challenge of seeing that justice was done in the courtroom. But he wondered: Was television's depiction of the legal profession true to life? What would it really be like to work as a lawyer?

One day he discussed this with an adult friend, who said, "I know some lawyers here in town. If you want, I can arrange for several of them to meet with you and tell you what it's like to practice law in the real world."

The teen took him up on that offer, and during the next few weeks he met with four local attorneys. They didn't talk much about dramatic courtroom scenes and tearful confessions by the guilty; they talked about drafting wills and helping to settle property disputes. For the first time, the young man saw that even the most helpful lawyer might never set foot in a trial court. He ended up changing his career plans.

Those four attorneys, like Glenn Leatherwood, were mentors.

Why Mentors?

As those two stories show, mentoring takes varied forms. It can involve a relationship of months or years—or just an hour. The common thread is influence.

The dictionary uses words like *counselor, coach,* and *guide* to describe what a mentor does. In a way, we parents are to be our teens' foremost mentors. That's what this whole book is about. But in this chapter I'm talking about mentors from outside the immediate family who can help our teens to dream in ways that we probably can't.

Family counselors Gary and Dr. Greg Smalley put it this way: "Mentors can be a powerful force . . . because 'outside instruction' can make a special impression on [teens'] lives. We're not suggesting that a parent's words no longer have an impact, but teens do seem more motivated to listen to those outside the family."[2]

Mentors can also give our kids insights into areas we know nothing about:

- The teen who needed counsel about lawyering couldn't have gotten it from his engineer father or his homemaker mother.
- John Maxwell's son, Joel, dreamed of one day running his own stage lighting business—a field in which John and his wife had no experience. But two men in John's church did, and they let Joel learn by laboring alongside them.
- A teen girl who dreamed of becoming a doctor found a cardiologist who allowed her to shadow him for several days—even witnessing open-heart surgery. Her single mom never could have provided that peek into the girl's potential profession.

Speaking of single parents, mentors can be especially helpful when you're raising a teen alone. Trustworthy mentors who take a personal interest in our kids can provide good role models and help to fill the void left by the missing parent.

Regardless of our marital status, though, mentors can be worth their weight in gold to us parents as we seek to help our teens dream.

How Mentoring Works

There are as many ways to mentor as there are people who can handle the job. Here are just three models to consider.

1. *The long-term friendship.* Barb met her youth pastor, Ron, when she was in junior high. In the years that followed, they talked often about faith, relationships, and life in general. Once in a while Ron and his wife would have Barb over for dinner.

Seeing leadership potential in Barb, Ron encouraged her to try new things and stretch herself. "I know you can do it," he'd tell her.

When Barb developed an interest, Ron helped her explore it and evaluate pros and cons. Later Barb would recall, "He believed in me . . . in my ability to follow the Spirit's leading and chart my own course in life—and that made me believe in myself."

After Barb graduated from college, Ron invited her to participate in a training program at the church he pastored. It wasn't easy, but "Ron talked it through with me. He helped me to find the positives in it. One . . . was that God used it to veer me in another career direction that was complementary but different from what I had planned."

Barb ended up in a career that let her do everything she'd dreamed of as a high school student. She concludes, "It all goes back to those days when Ron and I sat at the drugstore counter, having Cokes, while he said to me, 'Barb, you don't have to take a back seat in life because you're a woman.' It goes back to the way he encouraged me to be open to new things."[3]

2. *The short-term apprenticeship.* A mentoring relationship doesn't have to last years to be meaningful. Take Christian summer camp counselors, for example. At our Kanakuk sports camps, 2,500 collegiate and professional athletes who have a passion for helping kids mentor them every

year. Those influencers help kids determine what their dreams are, then guide them in pursuing those for two to four weeks of camp.

Afterward, follow-up seals the deal. Our counselors write, E-mail, and phone to encourage campers in their sports goals—and in their eternal objective of walking hand in hand with the Lord.

3. *The one-time interview.* When their daughter Bethany was 14, Tim and Pam Elmore asked six women that they and Bethany respected to serve as one-day mentors. During the next year, Bethany spent a day with each woman.

As Tim and Pam requested, the women discussed their "life messages" with Bethany. They also shared insights and expertise that might help Bethany think through her plans.

One of the women, Sarah, was a nurse. Since Bethany had been thinking about becoming a nurse midwife, Sarah took her to a maternity ward for the day. Bethany got to see a natural birth and a C-section, and she attended Sarah's class for unwed mothers. At the end of the day, Sarah talked to Bethany about sexual purity. Says Tim, "You can bet that went over way better than lecture 407 from Dad on that subject."[4]

Mentors Who Mark Milestones

Another way mentors can help our teens dream is to join us in creating ceremonies that instill a sense of purpose and vision.

When my son Cooper turned 16, I arranged for nine men who'd mentored him—teachers, coaches, family friends—to spend an evening staging such a ceremony for him. Each man carried a black Maglite; the theme for the night was "walking in the light." We held the ceremony outdoors, in the dark.

The first man met Cooper, put an arm around his shoulder, and walked with him slowly for about a hundred yards in the beam of the flashlight. As they walked, the man talked to Cooper about a character quality that would be important as Cooper passed from boyhood to manhood. About halfway to where the next man was waiting, the first man stopped, shined his light down the path ahead, and said, "Cooper, continue to walk in the light."

Cooper kept walking in that light beam until he came to the second man, who repeated the process, talking about another vital character trait. And so it went with all nine men; one focused on purity, another on integrity. Still another explained the concept of vision, of learning to discern God's leading and serving Him with the talents and passions we've been given.

The last man brought Cooper to a campfire, where his Grandpa Spike White and the whole gang of mentors waited. As we gathered around Cooper, his grandfather led us in a prayer of blessing for him. The men were saying, in effect, "If you ever need a friend, I'll be that friend. I will also hold you accountable to these character qualities that we've discussed. And I'll be praying for you."

As Cooper and I made our way home at the end of the evening, I asked how he was feeling. He replied, "You know what, Dad? It's going to take me a long time to be able to describe to you what this meant to me." It was clear that the experience had gone way, way down deep into his heart.

The Elmores, who arranged for their daughter Bethany to spend a day with each of six mentors, planned a similar ceremony for her at the end of that year. In this case, though, Bethany would do much of the talking. She would read to each woman a specific thank-you and explain "what I learned from you that day we spent together." Then all the women would lay hands on her and pray a blessing over her.

Another father asked his dad, who lived a thousand miles away, to take part in a small ceremony for his teen son the next time they were all together. When that time came, the grandfather spent an hour talking to his grandson about the lessons he'd learned in seven decades of walking with God. Then he prayed a blessing on his grandson.

Ceremonies like these can be a spiritual highlight of a teen's life, helping to fix in the child's heart a sense of identity and purpose in living for the Lord. The presence of mentors makes the events all the more special.

For more ideas about marking milestones with your kids, see the following books:

Spiritual Milestones, by Jim and Janet Weidmann and J. Otis and Gail Ledbetter (Cook Communications Ministries, 2001)

Raising a Modern-Day Knight, by Robert Lewis (Focus on the Family/Tyndale, 1997)

Where to Find Mentors

No matter what form mentoring takes, the key is to find adults who care enough for our teens to invest in their spiritual and vocational development. But where do we find such people?

Family members are a good place to start—grandparents, aunts, uncles, cousins.

At church, youth leaders or Sunday school teachers are strong possibilities. Your pastor might also suggest others in the congregation who would be a good match for your teen.

If your teen is involved with a group like Young Life or Fellowship of Christian Athletes, a leader or sponsoring parent there could become a great mentor. At school, a Christian teacher, coach, or guidance counselor might help.

Other potential mentors include family friends, parents of your teen's friends, co-workers, neighbors, and Christian camp counselors. When it comes to career insights, look to doctors, lawyers, plumbers, businesspeople, firefighters, computer programmers, auto mechanics—the experts in fields your teen may be considering.

>> "My high school teacher encouraged me in all areas of my life, from school grades to my music, to my faith and relationships. She still E-mails me to see how I am doing."

—*Jacob*

Focus on the Fun

At the 2002 Winter Olympic Games, the surprise winner in ladies' figure skating was teenager Sarah Hughes. She stunned the world by winning the long program and, with it, the gold medal. Asked how she'd been able to give the best performance of her life in the most-pressure-packed situation, she replied, "I just went out and had fun."

Setting goals and dreaming dreams may be serious business, but that doesn't mean it can't be fun. In fact, teens usually respond better to mentors who display a sense of humor than to those who make learning and practicing a grim chore.

A certain friend of mine is a good example. He's a college swimming coach and mentor to his team. His school didn't even *have* a swim team before he came, but he soon built a highly successful program. How? Through hard work—and making practice fun.

All day he would run around the pool with M & Ms. Every time a girl completed her laps in good time, he'd pop an M & M in her mouth. At first the swimmers thought it was pretty hokey. But when they found out that this guy was all about having fun, more and more kids came out for the team. Because the coach made it fun, they saw their athletic dreams come true.

Whenever possible, find mentors who focus on the fun. Teens who are big and effective dreamers say one reason for their success is that their parents focused on having fun rather than on "winning." Whether you're doing the mentoring yourself or relying on someone else, enjoying the journey can be more important than the destination. Then, as one teen says, "Winning is just icing on the cake."

Mentoring Other Teens

Just as our families can benefit from outside mentors, so we can also provide that helping hand to other parents and their teens. I've always figured it would be unfair for me to ask others to assist my kids if I wasn't assisting theirs. And that's led to some of the greatest experiences of my life.

When my older daughter was in ninth grade, I became concerned for her male friends—a bunch of great guys who just needed some encouragement in their faith. I challenged eight of them to come over to the house every Friday morning for doughnuts and Bible study. I became their outside-the-home mentor—and, to several of them, the only spiritual mentor they had. We ended up spending four years together!

After that I did the same thing with other groups of eight at a time, including my two sons' closest friends. Many of the kids met the Lord, and all grew in their relationship with Him.

Nothing's more fun than mentoring other people's kids, gathering them around a table, a Bible, and a couple dozen doughnuts. And now that those kids are in college and beyond, several still call and come by to discuss their most difficult decisions.

Please keep your eyes open, especially for kids who have single moms and don't have a male mentor—and children of single dads who don't have a positive female influence. Take them under your wing. You don't have to be a professional Christian counselor; I'm not. I'm just a layman who steps alongside other kids in the community.

The Lord says that if we cast off our crumbs, we're going to get back the whole loaf (see Ecclesiastes 11:1-2). I've found that as I look for kids to mentor, the Lord finds mentors for my kids, too. It just comes back to you.

Get the Mentor Mentality

Don't go it alone when it comes to helping your teen to dream. Find mentors who can assist in the process, and enlist their support.

As my next-door neighbors Gary and Norma Smalley declared, connecting your adolescent with Christ-centered mentors is the single best thing you can do for him or her outside the home. Your teen's ability to dream—and to dream well—will be much stronger for the experience.

// WITH YOUR TEENAGER

Over homemade fruit smoothies at the kitchen table, try the following:

- Using what you've read in this chapter, explain briefly some of the ways in which mentors might be able to help your teen.
- Ask: "Based on the current shape of your interests and dreams, how could you most use the assistance of a mentor?"
- Ask: "How could I, as a parent who loves you, be a better mentor to you?"

11

teaching your teen to see where God is at work

Try as they might, the shepherds found it difficult to see God at work in the world.

Little kids see themselves as the center of the universe. When they get a little older, they're shocked to discover that the human race has been going on for thousands of years. It began long before they arrived, and it will likely continue long after they're gone.

Teens tend to focus on themselves too:

- "What opportunities do *I* have?"
- "What can life offer *me?*"
- "How do *I* want to use the talents and gifts God gave *me?*"

- "What sort of work and lifestyle will make *me* happy and give *me* a sense of accomplishment or satisfaction?"

To be fair, this mind-set isn't limited by age. It often continues through the adult years as well.

It can be painful to admit that life isn't all about us. But as Rick Warren writes in *The Purpose-Driven Life*,

> It's not about you. The purpose of your life is far greater than your own personal fulfillment, your peace of mind, or even your happiness. It's far greater than your family, your career, or even your wildest dreams and ambitions. If you want to know why you were placed on this planet, you must begin with God. You were born *by* His purpose and *for* His purpose.[1]

And what is that purpose? Warren puts it simply: "The smile of God is the goal of your life."[2]

In other words, we and our teens are here to please our Creator. If that sounds like a crummy assignment, consider this:

> Bringing enjoyment to God, living for His pleasure, is the first purpose of your life. When you fully understand this truth, you will never again have a problem with feeling insignificant. It proves your worth.[3]

Jesus said, "For whoever wants to save his life will lose it, but whoever loses his life for me and for the gospel will save it" (Mark 8:35). This is God's wonderful paradox: In giving, we receive; by serving others, we're blessed; through putting our lives in His service, we find the greatest joy and fulfillment.

So how can our teens plan lives that please God? Henry Blackaby and Claude King, authors of *Experiencing God*, explain the situation this way:

God has been at work in our world. He is presently at work in our world. Because of His love He wants us to have the privilege of working with Him as His ambassadors. . . . His desire is to get us from where we are to where He is working. When God reveals to you where He is working, that becomes His invitation to join Him. . . . Your job as a servant is to follow Jesus' example: Do what the Father is already doing—*watch to see where God is at work and join Him!*[4]

To dream God-honoring dreams, our teens need to look not only at how they're wired—but also at how God is active in the world and how they might fit into what He's already doing.

As parents, it's our privilege to help them discover how to do that.

Learning to See God at Work

Hockey great Wayne Gretzky was once asked, "How do you always find yourself around the puck?"

"I don't go where the puck is," he answered. "I go where the puck is going to be."

In the same way, we want our teens to get good at seeing where things are headed—especially where God is busy and could have a role for them. To do that, we need to introduce them to the following four keys.

Key #1: Close Relationship

Discerning where God is at work starts with being in a close relationship with Him. As our teens get to know His nature and His ways, as they grow in the understanding that He loves them and *wants* to engage them in His work, and as they seek His guidance in prayer, He'll open their eyes to see more of what He's doing.

Connecting with God in this way has to come before our kids get wrapped up in their own plans, though. As Blackaby and King put it,

> Planning is a valuable tool, but it can never become a substitute for God. Your relationship with God is far more important to Him than any planning you can do. . . . Let God interrupt or redirect your plans anytime He wants. Remain in a close relationship with Him so you can always hear His voice when He wants to speak to you.[5]

Kent was a young man who had plans of his own—to report the daily news and expose corruption wherever he found it. He chose journalism as his college major.

But then he joined a Navigators Bible study. His understanding of God and love for Him grew by leaps and bounds. Gradually his perspective shifted; he still saw newspaper journalism as good and even vital, but he also came to realize that God might want him to help change hearts by spreading the Good News about Jesus Christ.

Eventually Kent decided that God was leading him into the field of Christian journalism. That doesn't mean God wouldn't lead someone else into "secular" reporting. It just shows how a closer connection with God helped one person develop a greater openness to His leading and a willingness to follow Him in a new direction.

Key #2: The Way They're Wired

Our teens can also learn to discern where God is at work by considering how He seems to be leading through their interests, abilities, and spiritual gifts. God does ask us to work outside our "comfort zones" sometimes, but He most often seems to lead according to our unique designs.

For example, He'll probably ask a teen who loves children to become a teacher rather than a computer programmer. The teen who loves algorithms, on the other hand, will more likely be led to design computer processors than to run a child care center.

Our kids need to ask themselves, "How has God equipped me with talents, abilities, and spiritual gifts? What interests and passions has He put in my heart? And how might those fit into what He's showing me about what He's doing in the world?"

My daughter Jamie discovered a way to serve God when she followed her heart and her talents. When she was five years old, I gave her a picture of a Cambodian child living in a Christian orphanage. Using her Christmas gift, Jamie began to support that child. She put the picture on her bulletin board and soon felt connected to the little girl.

By the time Jamie was 13, she'd developed a strong sense of compassion for needy people and an awareness of how God was using people like her to help the poor around the world. That's when, during a missions trip with me in the Caribbean, she got an idea for a line of clothes for teen girls using discarded cotton flour bags commonly found in the islands. She started a company to make and sell those clothes, and they were a hit. Dillard's, Nordstrom, and the Bass Pro Shops featured Jamie's company, White Sands, in stores across the U.S.

Over the next few years, to everyone's amazement, she made $300,000 in profit!

What did Jamie do with all that money? She gave away every penny to help hurting children in America and abroad. Her passion for the cause, for being part of God's work among the needy, combined with a talent for fashion design, led her to an opportunity that produced great physical and spiritual fruit.

Key #3: A Local Look

Where should our teens look next to find God at work? Right where they are.

We tend to think God is doing things "out there"—on some foreign mission field or through people in the public spotlight. But God is at work, and wants to be more involved, in the life of every follower of Jesus.

Encourage your teen to think about questions like these:

- "Do any of my friends, classmates, or teammates show an interest in spiritual questions, and could I help to point them in the right direction?"
- "Are there ways to serve in our church that might fit my interests and abilities? How about in our community? In my school?"
- "Could some new kid in my youth group or Fellowship of Christian Athletes huddle use some encouragement and friendship?"

Here's a simple pattern you can teach your teen:

- *Pray.* Only God knows what He has for you to do.
- *Look for a connection between your prayer and what might be an answer.* If you asked God for direction, does a friend start wondering aloud why you believe in heaven? Does your youth leader post a sign-up sheet for the next mission trip?
- *Ask questions.* Of people who cross your path: "Do you want to talk? How can I pray for you? What's the biggest thing happening in your life right now?" Of opportunities that arise: "Does this seem to fit with my skills and passions? Might God use this to make me stronger or to bring my goals and dreams into sharper focus?"[6]

›› "My mom has shown me Christian service with her life by volunteering and serving in areas in the community. Even when she wasn't doing something she loved, she was still willing to serve God."

—*Jessica*

Henry Blackaby recalls how, when he pastored a church in Saskatoon, Canada, he and some college students in the congregation wanted to start Bible studies in the dorms of a nearby university. For almost two years they tried to make it work, with little success.

One day he suggested to the students that, besides continuing to pray about the situation, they try something new: "This week I want you to go to the campus and watch to see where God is working and join Him. . . .

If someone starts asking you spiritual questions, whatever else you have planned, don't do it. Cancel what you are doing. Go with that individual and look to see what God is doing there."

That was on a Sunday. On the following Wednesday night, one of the female students said, "Oh Pastor, a girl who has been in classes with me for two years came to me after class today. She said, 'I think you might be a Christian. I need to talk to you.' . . . We went to the cafeteria to talk. She said, 'Eleven of us girls in the dorm have been studying the Bible, and none of us are Christians. Do you know somebody who can lead us in a Bible study?'"

Before long, there were three Bible studies going in the women's dorms, and two in the men's—because those young people looked for God at work right where they were.[7]

Key #4: The Wider World

In addition to looking locally, your teen needs to see what God is doing elsewhere. What might He be up to in your town, state, and country, and in other parts of the globe? How could your teen fit in?

One global trend, for instance, is urbanization. According to *National Geographic* magazine,

> In 1950 there was just one city with a population of ten million—
> New York. In 2015 there will be 21, and the number of urban areas
> with populations between five and ten million will shoot from 7 to 37.
> . . . Never have urban populations expanded so fast. . . . Worldwide,
> cities gain a million people a week.[8]

What could you and your teen do with that information? First, you could talk about the fact that God loves the people streaming into the world's cities. He wants to see their physical, emotional, and spiritual needs met. Then you could brainstorm ways in which your teen's passions, talents, and gifts might be put to use in a skyscraper, subway, or *barrio*.

Another trend is the Christian church's growth in the developing world, especially the southern hemisphere. Philip Jenkins, Distinguished Professor of History and Religious Studies at Penn State University, observes,

> It would not be easy to convince a congregation in Seoul [South Korea] or Nairobi [Kenya] that Christianity is dying, when their main concern is building a worship facility big enough for the 10,000 or 20,000 members they have gained over the past few years. And these new converts are mostly teenagers and young adults, very few with white hair.[9]

Faced with that information, not every teen will dream of becoming a missionary in Asia or Africa. But some will. And all of them will have the opportunity to consider how God might want them to support their brothers and sisters in those parts of the world.

Here are three more ways for your teen to keep up with what God is doing on planet earth:

1. *Watch the news.* TV reports, newspaper and magazine articles, Internet sites—all can keep your teen dreaming if she watches and reads with the "What is God doing?" question in mind.

2. *Talk with visitors.* When missionaries come to your church, attend their presentations or invite them over for dinner. Ask them what's really going on where they work and how your family can help.

3. *Go on a trip.* I can't recommend highly enough that teens take part in short-term missions trips. Nothing helps more to foster a vision-led teen. I'd go so far as to say that if you want to see Christ-centered dreams grow in your teen, at least one such trip in the high school years is a must. From personal adventures with my own kids and dozens of others whom I've taken to Haiti, I can promise you that their futures will be forever

changed. They'll never return completely to a me-centered, shortsighted lifestyle.

From Here to Eternity

Our teens don't have to plan their lives in a vacuum. The God who wired them is at work in our world. He invites them to be an exciting part of what He's up to. As Rick Warren puts it,

> God has a purpose for your life on earth, but it doesn't end here. His plan involves far more than the few decades you will spend on this planet. It's more than "the opportunity of a lifetime"; God offers you an opportunity *beyond* your lifetime.[10]

// WITH YOUR TEENAGER

Over a hot deep dish at your favorite pizza parlor, try the following:
- Using what you've read in this chapter, explain briefly what it means to look for places where God is at work—and how to find them.
- Ask: "What do you think God is doing in our town? How could you—or our whole family—get involved?"
- Ask: "Let's suppose you were interested in doing some kind of mission work in one of those bursting-at-the-seams cities in the developing world. Based on what you've learned so far about how God has wired you, what sorts of things might you want to do?"

12

helping your teen make decisions with long-term goals in mind

*Looking back, Heather regretted her decision
not to feed her pet python more often.*

More than any previous generation, today's teens are short-term, *now* thinkers. Christian pollster George Barna puts it like this:

> The dominant crises [for teens] are immediate and short term. That's the way teenagers think and live. . . . They are not overly concerned about things that may be significant problems eons from now—such as health and career decisions and opportunities.[1]

Today's kids have been called the Now Generation, because they want everything immediately. That's not so unlike previous generations, but it's more the case than ever in this day of Easy Mac instant macaroni and cheese. If they can't get instant success, kids get their video games out and create it in a virtual way.

Why do I point out this mind-set?

- Because a teen whose focus is entirely on the short term will be more concerned with what she's wearing to school tomorrow than with learning geometry or physics.
- Because a today-only thinker may drink beer or smoke pot at a party because it's the way to gain acceptance with the popular crowd.
- Because a teen seeking immediate gratification will want to spend every dime he makes (or is given) on clothes, music, and movies—rather than save toward college expenses or a missions trip.
- Because a teen who lives only for the here and now will be sorely tempted to become sexually active because it feels good and "everyone else is doing it."

The today-only mind-set is a challenge when we're trying to help our children dream God-honoring dreams about the future. Making those dreams come true takes planning, then pursuing those plans day by day—often without seeing short-term results.

How do we meet that challenge? How do we help our teens learn to make good decisions today, with eternal values and long-term goals in view?

Parental Example: The Starting Point

Our teens need to see eternal values and long-term thinking modeled by Mom and Dad. If, as we're making decisions, we seriously ask ourselves, "Will this honor God? Will this help us or hinder us in reaching our goal?" our children will learn to do the same.

Let's say you hope your teen will dream of having a godly marriage. If you're married, what kind of marriage are you modeling for him? Does he see you helping, supporting, encouraging, praying with, playing with, laughing with, serving with, and complimenting your spouse? Based on your example, does your teen consider long-term marriage to be worth short-term sacrifice?

My beloved dad—who was a dream-builder for his three boys, for sailors in the U.S. Navy, for students at Texas A & M, and for kids at Kanakuk Kamps until he went home to be with the Lord in early 2003—was a great marriage modeler. He never told me to "love your [wife], just as Christ loved the church" (Ephesians 5:25). But I'll never forget seeing the love notes he wrote to my mom almost every day through 66 years of marriage, nor the fact that I never, ever heard him say anything negative about her.

›› "Mom had such integrity and consistency that she was an example in leading me back to the Lord, which was the starting point of learning everything else."

—*Alan*

In the same way, Dad didn't have to tell me to care about overlooked people. Early every Monday and Friday morning, he would meet the men who collected our garbage and hand each of them a cup of hot coffee and a sweet roll. His favorite saying was, "I'd rather *see* a sermon than *hear* one any day." He lived that creed to the very end.

Our teens need to see us making short-term sacrifices for long-term goals. The way we handle money is a crucial example. Do we spend less than we earn and save the difference for things like retirement or our children's college education? Or do we spend every cent we make and borrow even more so we can have nice vacations and new cars today?

One husband and wife lived in their dream house—plenty of room, plus a back deck with gorgeous mountain views. But they wanted to serve God in missions work someday, and they knew that would be a lot easier if they didn't have a mortgage. After much prayer and discussion, they sold that house and put their equity into a smaller one whose mortgage could be paid off much sooner.

Their kids understood and supported the decision. They also learned a lot about making today's buying decisions in light of a bigger vision for tomorrow.

Keeping the Vision in View

With a jam-packed schedule of classes, homework, sports, sleepovers, youth group meetings, chores, and after-school jobs (not to mention all that eating and TV-watching), it's easy for a teenager to lose sight of the future. You can help by keeping a vision for that future in your teen's view. Whatever dreams she harbors, make them a regular topic of conversation in the car, at mealtimes, and at bedtime.

Your comments and questions can be as specific as the dream:

- "Is that the next math course you need for getting into engineering college?"
- "Can you do that after-school job and still train to make the varsity track team?"

Even if your teen's dreams are a bit nebulous, you can encourage the pursuit of such "inner" goals as strong character and living with no regrets:

- "I know you'd like to do things with that group of kids. But if they're pressuring you to drink, are those really the kind of friends who'll help you be the person you want to be, one who honors God?"
- "I'm proud of you for choosing to take that tough science class. It shows me you want to stretch yourself and develop to your full potential."

It's a challenge, of course, to do this without nagging. A lot of this has to do with the approach we use:

- Do we whine, complain, or try to dictate choices? Or do we cheer-lead, ask questions respectfully, and offer opinions *when requested?*

- Is most of what we say critical and second guessing, or is it affirming and relationship building?
- Do our teens expect a lecture every time we open our mouths, or do they anticipate compliments, expressions of love, and the occasional clarifying question or thoughtful suggestion?

When we sensitively encourage our kids to make daily decisions with lifelong goals in view—and model that behavior ourselves—they'll respond.

One Dreamer's Story

Agnessa is a young woman who learned to make today's choices with tomorrow in mind. Her dream was to serve God by becoming a medical doctor.

That meant skipping much of the high school and college social scene in order to study hard and do well in tough science classes. It meant sacrificing popularity to keep her mind clear and her morals high.

That might have been easy if Agnessa had been a supersaint who didn't care what others thought. But she wasn't. Like any teen, she wanted to be accepted and liked. Yet she wanted even more to honor God and to work toward the fulfillment of her dream.

Ask Agnessa how she managed to keep her focus and she'll give you five reasons—all of which trace back to the faith, values, and vision instilled by a devoted Christian mother:

1. "My mother had given my sisters and me a model of seeking God with your whole heart and mind. Because of her example and teaching, I embraced Him as my Father and really thought about what it means to please Him and ask for His protection and purity every day."

2. "I saw the situation in high school and college as a test of my ability to stand up for my beliefs, of whether I would fear God and not man. It was also a test of my independence—could I be my own person instead of going along with the crowd in order to be more popular?"

3. "Because I had a strong, loving relationship with my mom and sisters, I didn't have a void in my life that needed filling with drugs or sex. I also knew that those things had consequences that could ruin your life."

4. "My mom grew up in the old Soviet Union, where she was denied the opportunity to get a good education and have a meaningful career because of her Christian faith. After we moved to America, she made sure we realized how blessed we were and that we girls should take full advantage of all the opportunities we now had."

5. "I knew that high school and college wouldn't last forever."

With a pragmatic attitude that like, a world perspective, and the strength of a close relationship with family and the Lord, it's no wonder Agnessa didn't lose sight of her dream. At this writing she's still on track as a third-year student at the University of Colorado Medical School.

A Matter of Perspective

Like many of us, teens are naturally inclined to focus on the here and now. That's not all bad. But it can lead to decisions that betray their values and sabotage their pursuit of longer-term goals.

We can help them keep their visions in view. It takes modeling a healthy and God-honoring perspective, keeping the lines of communication open, and reminding them that some dishes are best prepared in a slow-cooker, not a microwave.

// WITH YOUR TEENAGER

Over a tall glass of iced tea or a mug of hot chocolate, try the following:

- Tell how a seemingly minor decision you made as a teen had a major, lasting impact on your life, either good or bad.
- Ask: "Have you ever seen me make a decision with a long-range goal in mind? What did I have to give up? Do you think it was worth it? How could I set a better example in that area?"

- Ask: "How well do you think you do at making decisions that support your dreams? What makes it most difficult for you to make wise choices?"

13

learning from life's scars

When life handed him lemons, Randy didn't just make lemonade

Teenager Natalie Foley was one of the U.S.'s top gymnasts. She'd dreamed of representing her country at the world championships, and she had put in years of hard work to turn that dream into reality.

All her effort was finally paying off. The national championships were just a week away, and then the top performers would compete for the United States at the World Championships in Belgium. To outward appearances, Natalie was poised to make a run for the gold.

The real picture, however, was anything but golden. "I was so pressured and nervous," Natalie recalls. "That day, with only a week to go to Nationals, I had a terrible practice. In the car on the way home, I cried and told God through my tears, 'I don't know why You're having me go through this!' I was breaking down, lacking confidence . . . [that] I could do it."

When she got home, "I talked with my dad, Steve, who had been an All-Pro defensive back for the Denver Broncos. He sat with me and listened while I poured out my heart. Then, finally, I asked him what I should do.

"What he shared with me was not things he had learned from all his successes and playing for NFL championships. Instead he shared his hurts—the times that he had failed, the times he had gotten cut from a team and been injured and how God had used his hurts for His bigger plan. Then he told me that I was such a blessing to be a daddy to, and he said, 'You have no idea how much I love you.'

"When Daddy told me those things, and I thought of my heavenly Father's unconditional love as well, I was free. I knew that no matter what happened at Nationals the next week, I couldn't fail. At that moment, I gave it up. I decided, 'This is no longer for me; this is for God. I'll let it go and let God. I'll simply do my best and let God do the rest.'"

As Natalie's story shows, even top performers encounter setbacks on the way to realizing their dreams. More importantly, it's a reminder that hard times can be opportunities for growth, for fine-tuning those goals.

Your teen will run into roadblocks, too. This chapter is about making the best of them.

Setbacks: A Part of Life

Most of us would like to protect our children from all pain, from detours and dead ends. We'd like their journey through life to be an unbroken string of successes. But life on this planet doesn't work that way, no matter how talented you are.

Consider the case of basketball great Michael Jordan. Were his skill and potential clear from the moment he first stepped onto a court? Not exactly. He was cut from his junior high basketball team.

How about best-selling novelist John Grisham? Did publishers and readers recognize his storytelling talent from the get-go? Nope. More than 20 companies turned down the chance to publish his first novel—and when it finally came out from a small, obscure publisher, the public didn't flock to snap it up. Only after his *second* book became a big hit did the first get much attention.

Then there was Abraham Lincoln. Did his brilliance as a leader and orator forge an endless chain of successes on his way to the White House? Not really. He lost far more elections than he ever won—and when he gave his now-famous Gettysburg Address, one of the finest presidential speeches ever, those in attendance called it only the *second*-best speech of the day.

The fact is that few dreams are reached on a smooth path. Stumbles, potholes, detours, and dead ends are the norm, not the exception. With God's help—and yours—your teen can understand that, expect that, and learn from those painful experiences.

Three Parental Responses

How can you help your teen cope with setbacks? Here are three suggestions:

1. *Acknowledge the hurt.* When your teen has a bad game or is cut from the team, doesn't get the part she wanted in the school play, does poorly on the college entrance exam, faces rejection by his friends because of his faith—you can be there with a soft shoulder to cry on and great big ears for listening.

When the setback happens, your teen doesn't want lectures and advice. He's hurting, and needs comfort and sympathy. As Steve Foley did after Natalie came home from that discouraging practice, you need to offer an affirming touch and listen, listen, listen.

Your teen may not ask for that. But he wants his parents to be the ones he can count on most. Moms and dads who don't respond can lose the privilege.

2. *Explain the pruning process.* After the initial waves of emotion have

subsided and your teen is ready to listen as well as talk, help her understand that setbacks and scars are not only normal—they're also part of God's pruning process. It's one way He causes us to grow and blossom, to know and serve Him better.

A good gardener knows that if bushes and trees aren't pruned, unwanted branches sap strength from the rest of the plant. So at just the right time, he snips off a branch. As a result, four more healthy branches may come out in better places and make the plant more beautiful and fruitful.

In the same way, God may prune our dreams. Sometimes it's to teach us humility and make sure praise goes to the right place. For example, I've seen many dads who think, *If I get my son on enough weights and feed him the right amount of protein and work him hard enough, he's going to be a great football player.* If that dream comes true without any setbacks, that father and son will be tempted to be proud—and God won't receive the glory.

A young man who suffers a season-ending injury or loses his spot as a starter, however, may come to appreciate the fact that his talent, health, and favor in the coach's eyes are all gifts from God.

3. *Look for a higher dream.* As your teen sorts through the aftermath of a disappointment, help her consider how the experience might be turned into an opportunity to pursue an even higher dream.

What do I mean? Natalie Foley, the young gymnast introduced at the beginning of this chapter, knows. Competing at U.S. Championships, she stood in third place entering the uneven parallel bars event. All was going well until, as she spun around on the high bar, her left grip came undone—forcing her to release the bar and fall to the mat for safety's sake.

The unfortunate timing of this equipment failure sent her to seventh place. All the hard work and self-denial ended, for the moment at least, in despair.

At the end of the day, as Natalie and her father drove away from the arena, she questioned why things would go so badly. Steve suggested, "Well, Natalie, let's go back to the big picture. What's the biggest goal in your life? Is it to be the top gymnast in the world?"

"No, Dad," she replied. "You know that it's to represent Christ and to trust Him in everything I do."

After praying with Natalie, Steve asked if she could see a way that God might use this defeat to help her achieve that goal.

"I suppose that if I just go out there with a positive attitude, give it my best, rely on the verse, 'I can do all things through Christ who strengthens me' and be content, no matter whether I fall or I give a perfect perform-ance, then people are going to see Jesus in that."

"You know," Steve concluded, "they're probably going to be able to see Him even more clearly in how you handle defeat than they are in how you'd handle winning."

God is surprising. Even when we pursue a dream with the best motives, thinking He'll get the glory when it comes true, He may have a detour in mind. He may come in the side door, not the front—causing things to go in a way you hadn't planned. But you discover that the result can be used even more to honor Him. You just stand there and say, "Wow! That has to be God."

Like Steve Foley, you can help your teen keep the bigger picture in view when things go "wrong," realizing that God may have something different and probably even better in mind. Even though gymnastics was very impor-tant to Natalie, it wasn't everything to her. She was able to put it all in per-spective. She even managed to find the positive in spite of the outcome. At times like these, the truth of Romans 8:28 ("And we know that in all things God works for the good of those who love him, who have been called according to his purpose") can be more than just a nice idea. It can become a real hope your teen can stake his life on.

Detour or Dead End?

When setbacks come, is it time for your teen to give up her dream? Not necessarily. Disappointment can be an opportunity to learn perseverance, to remember that no matter how badly things may have gone this time, there'll be another game and another season, another school play, another test, another project. Through adversity your teen can learn the value of discipline, practice, and paying the price for success.

To help your teen learn these lessons, ask questions that spur him to think. If he's played poorly in a basketball game, for example, you might ask later, when the emotions have subsided, "What can you learn from fouling out? How do you think that lesson could help you as a young CEO? How could it help you comfort others who are feeling down?"

>> "When a youth pastor speaking at a church camp was praying for me after hearing my struggles, he said something like this: 'I know You [God] are going to use Tim in great ways.' And that helps me see that God can use me in my weakness."

—Tim

Learning lessons may not be at the top of your teen's agenda, especially after disappointment. Many kids are ready to quit when things haven't gone their way. This may well be a time to reconsider goals, but it may also be a time calling for endurance.

One rule in our house is that the middle of the season—whether for a sport or the debate team or the drama production—is never the time to quit. That's when the initial excitement has worn off, things may not be going as well as the teen had hoped, and it's easy to get downhearted. That's also the time when it's most difficult for a person to be objective and make a clear-headed decision.

What *is* clear is that the teen has made a commitment to the team, coach, teacher, youth pastor, fellow cast members, or whoever else is involved. Keeping one's commitments is a core value that not only helps a child get through the trials of adolescence, but it also prepares him not to drop out of college when things get tough or to divorce when he hits rough waters in married life.

When the season is over or the commitment is otherwise fulfilled, then the teen can evaluate the experience and decide whether to keep going in the same direction.

In making that choice, the top priority for both teen and parent should be to pray about it. The biblical book of James encourages us, "If any of you lacks wisdom, he should ask God, who gives generously to all without finding fault, and it will be given to him" (1:5). God wants our teens to be wise about how they invest their time and energy; they and we can ask with confidence that He will guide.

The second priority is to listen to what the teen is saying. Perhaps the two of you have dreamed that she would become a champion gymnast like Natalie Foley, but now your daughter is saying, "I'm just not enjoying it anymore. I think I'd like to try volleyball." Maybe your son dreamed of becoming an artist, but lately he's saying, "I've done my best in art class, but I can see now that I just don't have the talent. I think I'd like to try out for the debate team."

If your teen has put a strong effort into pursuing an interest and kept her commitments, but now she thinks she'd like to go in a different direction, it may be time to let her quit gracefully.

On the other hand, if she wants to try again in spite of disappointment, the wise course may be to encourage that perseverance.

Middle schooler Lauren Hauschild came to our Kanakuk sports camp one summer because she loved to run and swim. While here, she noticed a small pain in her leg. When she went home the pain continued, so her parents took her to the doctor. The cause: bone cancer. Surgeons had to remove Lauren's leg.

At that point, most kids would have given up on any athletic dreams— at least those requiring the use of their legs. But 12-year-old Lauren didn't quit, and Mom and Dad cheered her on. They took her to endless physical therapy sessions, helped her adjust to life with a prosthetic, and encouraged her to push herself to do everything that others her age were doing.

Two years later, a teenaged Lauren was back at Kanakuk, taking the triathlon specialty! That's the sport requiring competitors to swim, run a long distance, and bicycle an even longer distance—all in the same race. That was the goal she'd set for herself, the dream that drove her through rehab. There she was, praising God and working up a sweat with a smile.

In two-parent homes, there's often one parent who's ready to let Johnny quit at the first hint of unhappiness; the other wants Johnny to grit his teeth and keep going. Such parents would do well to talk openly with each other, with Johnny, and with God.

Perhaps the more "merciful" parent needs to recognize that Johnny is learning the value of keeping commitments. Maybe the more hard-driving parent needs to accept the fact that Johnny will never be the next Joe Montana. Or it might be that God wants to take Johnny in a new direction that neither parent had considered.

Scars: A Source of Pride

Pursuing dreams leaves its scars. But scars can be a badge of honor.

All great athletes have scars. What's more, they're proud of them. The scars prove they're "real" athletes—tough enough to get knocked down and get back up again.

A Colorado teen named Matt has such a scar—and reason to be proud of it.

In 1999 Matt was a runner, artist, actor, musician, and top-notch student who dreamed of using those abilities in a life of service to God. Then two minutes threw all that into question.

Matt and his parents were driving to the Midwest to spend Christmas with family. But their car hit a patch of black ice, slid out of control, and slammed into a tractor-trailer parked beside the road. Moments later their car was T-boned by a pickup truck whose driver had also lost control.

Matt suffered a traumatic brain injury, along with a two-inch cut on his forehead. His short-term memory, coordination, and most of his self-control were gone. Soon his parents found he could fly into a violent rage without warning.

Matt's dreams had turned to question marks. Would he ever be able to take care of himself? Could his parents ever leave him alone again? Would he ever return to school?

A few weeks later, with help from good doctors and therapists, God did a miracle in Matt's mind. The "fog" cleared; the coordination, self-control, and ability to think and remember returned. Soon the only obvious reminder of his injury was that two-inch scar—a scar in which Matt took considerable pride.

The scar was evidence of what he'd been through. And when people asked about it, Matt told them about God's goodness. When technicians at the photo studio airbrushed the scar out of Matt's senior picture, he was indignant!

Matt is still proud of that scar. And he's back to pursuing God-honoring dreams, thankful for the second chance he's been given.

As your teen works toward his dreams, he'll suffer scars—physical, emotional, or both. But you can show him how God uses these for His purposes and your teen's good.

Someday your teen will be on the other side of these trials. That's when he'll be able to show his scars with pride—and tell stories of God's faithfulness.

// WITH YOUR TEENAGER
Over sundaes at your local ice cream shop, try the following:
- Using what you've read in this chapter, describe briefly how good can come out of disappointments and defeats. Relate a story of how you've experienced this in your own life.
- Ask: "What has been your biggest disappointment over the past couple of years? Can you identify anything you've learned from it— like being more patient, persistent, or compassionate toward others who are hurting?"
- Ask: "What goal or dream are you having problems with right now? How can I help you deal with those struggles?"

part four

where do you go from here?

»

14

giving whatever it takes

Though he had not fully investigated the details, Gary was convinced he would attend the college of his choice on a Nintendo scholarship.

When my son Brady was in middle school, he dreamed of being the starting shooting guard on his high school basketball team. As soon as he made that desire known, I determined to help make it come true.

Brady needed a little more time to practice than some of the other kids. My plan was to make sure he got all the practice he needed. That meant helping him find places to shoot baskets at night—and rebounding his shots for hour after hour, evening after evening.

Obviously, this required a major time commitment on my part. It meant *not* doing a lot of other things I could have done with my nights. It also meant finding the energy, after a long workday, to track down and pass back shot after shot. And, since there was no YMCA or health club nearby that we could join, it meant tracking down places where Brady could practice.

Because I was committed to helping Brady realize his dream, however, I was prepared to do whatever it took.

The good news is that all our hard work paid off. Brady's skills grew steadily, and eventually he was indeed a starting guard on his high school team. He got to enjoy the thrill and bear the agony of making and missing potential game-winning shots. And I got the satisfaction of building a great friendship with my son and being a key part of the dream come true.

For all of us who want to help our teens dream, a similar commitment is needed. Aiding them in finding out how they're wired is the beginning. But then, as I found with Brady, we need to make the commitment to do whatever it takes to help make the dreams come true.

Just what *will* it take? At least five different kinds of investments may be required: time, energy, resources, creativity, and humility. Let's look briefly at each.

Investment #1: Time

Between Brady's fourth and eleventh grades, I spent almost 1,000 hours with him in various gyms, rebounding and returning over 100,000 shots. I could have spent that time relaxing in front of the TV, reading the newspaper, or pursuing a hobby. But Brady and his dream became my hobby. I was building a basketball player—and, more significantly, a relationship.

In the same way, Ray and Rose Chavez of Albuquerque, New Mexico, poured countless hours into helping their five children excel in school and eventually graduate from one of America's most prestigious universities. Though both parents worked outside the home, they made the time to read to their kids and introduce them to music, math, and geography, and to take them to lessons and enrichment programs.

At one point, Rose took a night job so she could be home with the children during the day, encouraging and tutoring them. She comments now, "We were all in this together. We all worked to make it happen."[1]

Your teen's dreams may cost you time—perhaps many hours over the next few years. But every minute you spend will be an investment in your child's future, and in your relationship.

Investment #2: Energy

Working with your teen toward a goal, whether in a gym or at the dining room table, is going to take a lot of energy. Unfortunately, at the end of a long and challenging workday, our emotional and physical gas tanks are approaching empty. What strength we have left is needed for household chores and bill paying.

So how can we find the energy? I struggled with that issue until I came up with what I call the 10 Percent Rule. Here's how it works:

I set a goal to save 10 percent of my best energy for after five o'clock, when I left the office. I wouldn't give every drop of strength I had at work and come home dead tired. I would conserve my best for the family. When I came home, I had 10 percent left—energy for fun with the kids.

> ›› "Mom went on walks and listened to my passions and desires in life—with the underlying assumption that if God leads me into it, I can do it!"
>
> — *Christine*

During the day, I'd think about how I was going to spend that 10 percent. If I got home before the kids did, I'd be waiting with a football or basketball in my hand. I'd give that 10 percent, and it was good stuff. We had great times together.

A mom or dad in any line of work can adopt the 10 Percent Rule. It doesn't matter whether you're an office employee, factory worker, gardener, or executive.

Another good way to approach this challenge is to think of each day as a marathon to be run.

The marathon is a tough, long race—more than 26 miles. Knowing that, a marathoner paces himself to make sure he'll be able to finish and finish strong. He could sprint away from the starting line, going all out for 400 yards or even half a mile. But he knows that if he does that, his energy will be depleted long before he approaches the finish line. So he maintains a steady rate for 26 miles, holding power in reserve for a final kick when the race's end comes into view.

In a similar way, if my finish line is five o'clock and I pour out all my energy before that, when 5:01 hits I'm going to be dead tired. Instead, I think, *This isn't a sprint, this is a marathon. My finish line is not five o'clock, it's 9:30.* With that mind-set, I can hold that 10 percent in reserve and be excited to spend it at home.

If you saved 10 percent of your energy each day to help your teen pursue a dream, what might be accomplished? Try it! You could be amazed at the results.

Investment #3: Resources

Pursuing dreams costs money, too—perhaps a lot of it. If your budget is tight, you've got a lot of company—most of the other parents reading this book!

So where do you find the resources to fund dreams? The Chavez family of New Mexico had to answer that question repeatedly. Scholarships were only a partial help in sending their five kids to a top private high school and then an Ivy League university.

The simple answer is that Ray and Rose made funding their kids' education a top priority—then made decisions and sacrifices to pay the bills. For example, "We've always had just one car," Ray says. "For a couple of years, I bicycled five miles to work and back every day."

Rose adds, "We ate a lot of peanut butter and jelly sandwiches for lunch."

Ray and Rose also refinanced their home mortgage six times to cover tuition expenses. In the early years, believing that music lessons and learning to play an instrument would help the children, Rose took $10,000 from her retirement account to buy a baby grand piano for them.

Rose concludes, "We've read articles about families whose kids get accepted to good schools, then the parents say, 'We can't afford it—we're only middle class.' You can't have everything. You can't have a big car and a big vacation. You have to decide what's important."[2]

What are your financial priorities? I hope that helping to make your teen's dreams come true is at or near the top of your list, and that you're prepared to act accordingly.

Let's say you love to play golf, but it's expensive. So maybe you don't play for a few years in order to have more resources to spend on your kids' dreams. Or maybe you don't replace the old car for another year, or you replace a nice one with something less fancy to lower your payments and free up some cash every month.

Like time and energy, money put toward your teen's dreams is an investment, not just an expense. Combined with elbow grease, it can buy experience, skills, and self-confidence. Parents who send their athletically minded children to Kanakuk Kamps, for instance, often declare that their kids' registration fee was the finest investment they ever made.

What dividends might your teen and your family receive, now and in the future, from your investments in her dreams?

Investment #4: Creativity

Helping our teens pursue their dreams often requires a little creativity. I found this out when my son Brady needed all that basketball shooting practice, even in the winter and at night, when outdoor courts weren't usable. At the time our small town had no YMCA or other indoor gym facility open to the public in the evening.

Here's what I did. I identified institutions that had gyms that might be unused on a given night—elementary and middle schools, high schools, and colleges. Next I went to those places, located a friendly administrator or janitor, struck up an acquaintance, made our need known, and asked for permission to use the facilities.

Each time Brady and I wanted to practice, we'd make the rounds of those places until we found one where a janitor or administrator could let us in. We almost always found a place to shoot baskets.

How could creativity help your teen pursue a dream? Here are some ideas to get you thinking:

- Does your teen need the use of an Internet-ready computer, but you can't afford a new one? Perhaps you could borrow one from your workplace or buy an older one the next time your employer upgrades. Most public libraries also offer Internet access, as do some restaurants and coffee shops.

- Is your teen interested in exploring the possibility of missions work, but you don't know where to begin? Check out the Web sites of some mission organizations (for recommendations, ask your pastor or church missions committee). Most missionaries, active or retired, would be happy to correspond via E-mail or snail mail with an interested teen. When missionaries visit your church, invite them to lunch or dinner and let your teen ask questions.

- Does your teen think she might want to be a college soccer coach, but the only sport you know is tennis? Ask your high school coach about the training needed. A college coach probably would be happy to meet with your teen and might even let her hang around and help out during practices. A reference librarian could direct you to printed information about the requirements for and pay scales in various occupations. While you're there, look for books on how to be a successful soccer coach.

When obstacles seem to limit your ability to help your teen pursue a dream, apply a little creativity of your own and see what happens. Persistence and old-fashioned shoe leather may be needed, but in the end you could be pleasantly surprised.

Investment #5: Humility

When it comes to helping your teen realize a dream, nothing beats a large dose of humility. There will be some things you can't do or provide; then it's time to ask for assistance.

- If your teen needs a place to shoot baskets, you might have to ask a janitor for help.
- If your teen needs money for a school or sports camp or missions trip, you may need to apply for a scholarship.
- If your teen needs tutoring in a subject to which you're a stranger, you might have to ask a more knowledgeable acquaintance to step in.
- If your teen's dream includes involvement in afternoon performances like band concerts or football scrimmages, you might need to ask your boss for time off so you can attend.

Humbling yourself can be difficult. But if you're determined to help your teen dream and see those dreams become reality, it's a cost you'll be willing to bear.

Worth It All

Becoming a dream facilitator for your teen will be costly. A "whatever it takes" attitude is required, not optional.

But the return on your investment of time, energy, resources, creativity, and humility will be priceless. It's the way to a great relationship with a teen who's excited about life and its possibilities and ready to tackle new dreams with confidence and passion.

// WITH YOUR TEENAGER

Over a Saturday breakfast at your favorite pancake place, try the following:

- Tell your teen you're committed to doing whatever you can to help in the pursuit of his or her dreams. Based on what you've read in this chapter, explain briefly what that might mean in terms of time, energy, resources, creativity, and humility.
- Ask: "What's the number one dream or goal you'd like to pursue right now? Why?"
- Ask: "What kinds of support do you most need from me to go after that dream? What would be the greatest help I could offer?" If your teen doesn't have immediate answers, give him or her a week to think about it.

15

getting mom and dad to work together

Mr. and Mrs. Armstrong's dreams for their son Stretch differed in small but significant ways.

Mike Harris, a high school junior, has suffered a wrestling injury—a separated shoulder. Already he's missed a couple of meets because of it, and he's eager to get back on the mat. He made all-state last year as a sophomore, and he knows the college recruiters are watching him closely with scholarship offers in their back pockets.

Dad is 100 percent behind Mike's dream. They both love wrestling; Dad was all-conference himself in his high school days. Dad also knows that a full-ride scholarship is the only way Mike will be able to attend college without piling up a small mountain of debt.

Mom, however, thinks Mike may need to give up his wrestling dreams and concentrate on academics. This is his third injury in two years, and she's read about injured athletes who are hobbled and in pain for the rest of their lives. Besides, if Mike doesn't start raising his GPA, he won't get into a good college no matter how many pins he gets on the mat!

Not surprisingly, there's a lot of conflict in the Harris household. Dad thinks Mom is too cautious and pessimistic and will ruin Mike by babying him. Mom thinks Dad is too driven and blind to the dangers and will ruin Mike by getting him crippled and letting him flunk out.

Mike, who tends to side with Dad but doesn't want to hurt Mom's feelings, feels torn between the two.

The Harris family is fictional, but it represents a lot of families in which parents don't see eye-to-eye about their teens' dreams. Getting caught in the middle isn't going to help a teen reach his or her goals.

If Mom and Dad Harris can learn to complement each other and provide a balanced perspective on Mike's situation, he and they will benefit. They'll be able to discuss the issues more productively and arrive at solutions that give Mike a green light to pursue God-honoring dreams.

The Power of Teamwork

As I sit here writing in my office, I see a flight of Canada geese soaring high overhead. These cross-continental flyers almost defy belief as they travel more than 2,000 miles between Canada and the Gulf of Mexico twice a year. How do they do it?

The key to their success is their ability to work together. Flying in their V formation, they take turns in the lead, breaking the wind for one another and drafting off each other's wings, just like race car drivers. Scientists have found that geese flying together can go a full 70 percent farther in a day than a single bird flying alone.

That reminds me of another amazing demonstration of the power of teamwork, this one put on at the 1893 Chicago World's Fair. A little mule was harnessed to a crushing load of 8,000 pounds. To the crowd's amazement, the small beast of burden dug in his hooves and pulled that sled across the dusty ground.

A second little mule was brought out, and this time the load was increased to 8,800 pounds! As the stunned audience watched, the small animal duplicated the pulling feat of the first mule.

Finally, the two were harnessed together and hitched to the sled. The crowd buzzed with anticipation. How much could the two beasts pull jointly? Maybe 16,000 pounds? 18,000? Even, incredible as it seemed, as much as 20,000 pounds?

The weights were piled on, the mules pulled the sled over the rough ground, and still more weights were added. First 16,000 pounds . . . then 18,000 . . . 20,000 . . . 25,000 . . . and finally 30,000 pounds! That's how much more the animals could do in tandem compared to what either could do alone.

Like the mules and the geese, moms and dads pulling together can have a far greater effect than either working separately—let alone at cross purposes.

My wife and I found out how true this is when our daughters were three and five years old. Like their mom before them, they were doing front rolls and cartwheels all over the house. I bought a used trampoline and made a short, carpeted balance beam that went in the family room, but we needed a gym! In our little town of Branson, Missouri, though, there was no facility for aspiring gymnasts.

Debbie Jo and I came up with the solution. Combining my capacity for wild dreaming with her logic and organizational skills, we built on paper a Christian gymnastics school for our community.

Three months later, Morning Star Gymnastics was bustling with dozens of tiny bodies dressed in leotards of all colors, leaping and rolling and springing across the floor. Soon we had a team and weekend stars in the making. For the next five years we trained and traveled, celebrated victories, worked through defeats, and built lifetime friendships.

That kind of parental teamwork goes a long way toward helping a teen to bring his or her dreams to life.

Seeds of Conflict

So what goes wrong? Why are husband-wife battles over a teen's dreams all too common? Here are four possible reasons:

1. *Personality clashes.* Everybody in relationships seems to have a little fleshy motivator that says, "I wish you were more like me. Why don't you see and feel things the way I do?"

Mom Harris, the nurturer, says to herself, *I wish my husband wasn't so pushy. I wish he was more like me.*

Dad Harris, the aggressive athlete, tells himself, *I wish my wife wasn't so overprotective. I wish she was more like me.*

We all know wives and husbands can be vastly different. For example, I'm spontaneous; I'll start up a new project without a moment's notice, only to drop it as soon as it's rolling so I can find something else to pursue. Debbie Jo, on the other hand, is the ultimate planner and organizer; once she starts something she'll stick with it through fire and storm until it's finished.

Opposites attract—and that's okay. But when opposites *attack*, there's a problem.

2. *Finding adult faults in the child.* Sometimes we react against something in our teen that we don't like in our spouse or in ourselves. Mom Harris, for example, may believe Dad could have been more successful if he'd studied harder in college and devoted less time to the wrestling team. Now, perhaps without even being aware of it, she may be determined that their son is not going to repeat his father's mistake.

Dad Harris, for his part, may regret quitting college wrestling after an injury. How far might he have gone in the sport if he'd just been a little tougher? Now, without realizing it, he may be determined that Mike is not going to repeat *that* mistake.

3. *Blasts from the past.* Memories of failure may cause one parent to have a hard time saying yes to a teen's dream. Maybe Mom Harris's own teenage dream of becoming a ballerina ended in disappointment. She came to believe that all such dreams end in pain. She wants desperately to spare her son the agony she went through.

4. *Conflicting values or priorities.* One parent, more overprotective than the other, may be willing to let a teen quit in the middle of an activity or commitment—while the other believes in toughing it out. One parent may think the coach or faculty adviser or employer is a jerk and will never give the child a fair chance, while the other thinks the teen has to learn how to deal with such situations on his or her own. Or one parent thinks the child's happiness is most important, while the other thinks keeping one's word is the top priority. In any case, conflict ensues.

Learning to Work Together

If you and your spouse have a hard time with teamwork, what can you do?

The key is to remember that you *are* a team. God has brought you together to blend your personalities and gifts and experiences. The husband completes the wife; she completes him. Rather than complain about the differences, you can value and learn from them.

This means respecting your mate's gifts and makeup. It means allowing your spouse's perspective to complement yours, like a hand sliding into a glove—rather than thinking you should both be "gloves." It means talking things through and really listening to each other, as opposed to talking *at* each other and cranking up the volume on the same old arguments time after time.

> ›› "Many times we'll sit down together, just my parents and I, and talk. I'll share what I desire to do in the future, and they will add their input and bring up aspects of my personality that I'm usually not considering."
> —*Heather A.*

It also means showing respect for and building up your mate in front of your teen, even if you're not yet seeing eye-to-eye. Bite your tongue if necessary to keep from undercutting or dishonoring your spouse in your child's presence. Parental disagreements are to be resolved in private.

Let's look at how this might play out in the Harris household.

Mike's shoulder is getting back into wrestling condition. He's hoping to start competing again in a couple more weeks, but Mom and Dad still don't agree on whether he should.

Over dinner one night, Mike talks excitedly about how well his rehab is going. Mom and Dad make eye contact, giving each other a look that says, "We need to come to some resolution on this." So, when Mike goes off to do his homework, the two of them head to their bedroom for a closed-door conversation.

"Look," Dad begins, "I know we've had some heated arguments about this, and we both have strong opinions. But I also know we're in this together, and for Mike's sake we need to work this out. So tell me again what you think we should do and why."

Mom explains her concern about Mike's grades. Dad nods and agrees that they need to help Mike balance athletics and academics. They decide to talk with him about that this weekend.

Mom then describes her worries about Mike's injuries. Dad says he understands but that injuries are "just part of the game." Still, he suggests that the three of them sit down with Mike's doctor and talk about Mike's condition and how he might prevent future injuries.

Next Dad talks about how Mike loves wrestling; this isn't something he was pushed into. Mike really wants to see how good he can be and how far he can go in the sport. Mom concedes that it's Mike's dream, that wrestling has given him a focus and work ethic he'd never had before, and that it's led him to join his school's Fellowship of Christian Athletes huddle.

Dad reflects on how a wrestling scholarship is Mike's best shot at college—if he can get his grades up. Mom reluctantly admits that's true.

As the conversation continues, both parents start to relax. They're seeing that though their perspectives may differ, they're on the same team, with the same love for their son.

Finally, they agree that giving Mike clear standards for study times and grades will help him do better in class—and that consulting the doctor will minimize his chances of serious injury as he returns to competing. A hug and a kiss seal the deal.

The Complementary Coopers

My friend Dr. Kenneth Cooper, the famed physician and fitness expert, told me his parents had very different views of his dreams. But both contributed to Ken's success—each in his or her own way. I'll let him tell the story:

My family said that I started talking about becoming a physician at approximately five years of age. I don't recall that distinctly, but during my early teens I was convinced that medicine was a profession I wished to pursue. In fact, during those early years I had two dreams: (1) to become a well-known physician and (2) to participate in the Olympic Games as a representative of the U.S.A. Unfortunately, I did not achieve the latter goal, but I have to some extent achieved the former.

During those formative years, my mother was my number one supporter of athletic activities. I won the one-mile run in the [1949] state championship in Oklahoma . . . and made all-state in basketball. My mother never missed one of my athletic events in high school, and even while [I was] on a track scholarship to the University of Oklahoma, she rarely missed one of my events in college.

To the contrary, my father, a busy, practicing dentist, had great concern about my participation in athletics, being afraid that I would end up with "an athletic heart." A popular concept during the '40s and early '50s was that your heart would enlarge if you exercised too much, and once you stopped exercising you would have a marked increase in risk for having a heart attack. Later, we were able to show that this concept was strictly a myth—no damage is done to a normal heart in response to a highly competitive exercise/sports program, and once you stop competing this does not increase your risk of a heart attack, and the enlarged heart reverts back to normal. . . .

Even though my father did not support my athletic endeavors, he strongly encouraged me to accomplish the most I could in my academic work. If I was going to be accepted into medical school, I must have good grades in both high school and pre-med. There was nothing he would not do for me to help reach that goal. . . .

I dedicated my first book, *Aerobics*, to my father, "who instilled in me an overwhelming desire to study and practice the art of preventive medicine," and to my mother, "who encouraged me in my athletic endeavors during the formative years."

. . . I am convinced that I would not have achieved at least the "dream" of becoming a physician if it had not been for the support of my parents—nor would I have achieved athletic success, even though this did not include making the Olympic team, without the support of my mother.

When a mom and dad complement each other like that, despite differing perspectives, there's no telling how far their teen can go.

// WITH YOUR TEENAGER

Over steaming cups at your local java joint, try the following:
- Based on what you've seen in this chapter, and showing respect and honor for your spouse (if you're married), acknowledge a difference between the two of you regarding your teen's dreams. (Note: This is *not* an opportunity to put down your spouse or try to make your-

self look better in comparison to him or her.) Explain how the two of you will work together to support your teen's dreams despite that difference.

- Ask: "How much do your father/mother and I seem to be on the same page when it comes to supporting your dreams? Are we giving you any mixed messages that are creating confusion?"
- Ask: "What's the best thing your father/mother and I could do, in terms of working together, to help you pursue your dreams?"

16

making sure it's your
teen's dream, not yours

*Sometimes Roger wondered whether his son truly shared
his dream that the boy would become a librarian.*

Jeff Johnson (not his real name) had a great arm, a great intuitive under-standing of football, great instincts under pressure on the field, and great natural athletic ability. He used those talents to build an All-American college career and make himself into a top pro prospect at quar-terback. And indeed, when the time came, an excited NFL team made him its first-round draft pick.

All the while, Jeff was miserably unhappy.

He tried to cover the pain with out-of-control activities that got him in repeated trouble. The pattern began during his college days, when he was living on his own for the first time. That made the pro scouts anxious, but his "one of the best ever" talent was too great to ignore.

The pattern only grew worse in his rookie NFL year, when he moved farther from home and had lots of money to blow. Drinking, reckless driving, showing up unprepared for practices—these were just some of the actions that soon made the team regret its choice. Before he knew it, Jeff's once-promising career came to an inglorious end.

What had gone wrong?

Simply put, the dream of football stardom and NFL greatness was his father's, not Jeff's. Dad's desire to achieve vicarious success through his son was so strong that he drove Jeff relentlessly, turning him into a "human doing" rather than a human being.

When Jeff did outstanding things on the field and his team won, Dad treated him like a champ. When the boy made mistakes and the team lost, he was in Dad's doghouse at least until the next game. Dad's acceptance was tied entirely to Jeff's performance.

Sadly, budding Jeff Johnson stories can be seen everywhere today. Go to any Little League baseball game, Pee Wee soccer contest, or high school basketball game and you're likely to see parents shouting things that would start brawls in any other setting. Officials, coaches, and the kids themselves are the targets of incredible verbal abuse. It happens with boys' and girls' teams, at public schools and Christian schools.

The same impulse can be seen, if manifested more quietly, at stage productions, music or dance recitals, art or academic competitions, and chess meets. Regardless of the setting, parents are pushing their kids to fulfill Mom or Dad's dreams.

A Matter of Life or Death

My name for pushy, demanding, never-satisfied, trying-to-live-through-their-kids parents is "mule drivers." Their method for getting what they want is to crack the whip. And when things don't go their way, the whole world is likely to hear about it—often in unprintable language.

Kids hate to be driven like mules. The older they get, the more they hate it, especially in the teen years. Not surprisingly, they may also grow to hate the mule driver.

Mule drivers may be frustrated by what they perceive as their own lack of accomplishment. They may have dreamed of finding stardom in sports, music, or some other field, only to discover that they didn't have the talent or didn't get the right break. They may not have had a secure relationship with a parent and are still living out that insecurity through their children.

Whatever the reason, these parents are re-creating the Jeff Johnson story over and over.

Trying to force our dreams on our kids is a formula for disaster. That's why we need to pursue something else: being the fragrance of life to our teens.

The concept comes from 2 Corinthians 2:15-16, which says, "For we are . . . the aroma of Christ among those who are being saved . . . the fragrance of life." When we're truly advancing our teens' dreams—not pushing our own—we will be the fragrance of life to them.

When the apostle Paul wrote that passage, his first-century Corinthian audience understood it well. When a conquering Roman general returned home and marched into the city with his troops and prisoners, he would also burn sweet spices whose fragrance filled the air.

To the people of Rome, that aroma was the smell of victory and life. To the prisoners, who knew they would soon face execution, it was the smell of defeat and death.

We can be to our teens either a fragrance of life or a fragrance of death. If we're genuinely working to help them realize their dreams, we'll be an aroma of life. But if we're pushing them to pursue *our* dreams, we'll be the smell of death.

Let's smell of life.

Death and Life Examples

One young woman wanted a medical career, but she couldn't decide whether to become a nurse or a doctor. Finally, because she felt more comfortable in a supporting role and didn't want the added stress of being a physician, her dream took shape: She would train to be a nurse.

That wasn't her father's dream, however—and he let her know it! He wanted her to pursue the prestige and paycheck of a doctor. "He shed a bad light on being in a more 'serving' position, which is where I like to be," she said.

That dad's intentions may have been good, but he ran roughshod over his daughter's dream. In the process, he became to her the fragrance of death.

In contrast, another young woman I know is on her way to great success as a golfer. Strangely enough, she wants her dad right beside her as her caddy—even though many players want family members to keep their distance on the course in order to maintain their concentration.

Why is this girl different? Because her dad is an encourager, a cheerleader—not a critic or a mule driver. The dream is hers, and he's there to help. He's the fragrance of life to her.

>> "My dad would say comments such as 'I don't know how you do that!' . . . Through the affirmation of my ' ventures,' I gained confidence to try even more things."

—*Christine*

A greeting card commercial pictured this aroma beautifully. A young girl, a figure skater, was about to have her turn on the ice in a big competition. Before she went out, her mom gave her two cards. The envelope holding one said, "In case you win." The other said, "In case you lose."

Curious, the girl opened the "winning" envelope. The card inside said something like, "I love you and I'm so proud of you." The girl smiled. Then, even more curious, she opened the "losing" envelope. The message on the card inside was the same: "I love you and I'm so proud of you."

Win or lose, that girl was loved and honored by her mother. That woman was to her daughter the fragrance of life.

Whose Dream Is It, Anyway?

No matter how good our intentions are, it's easy to slip into the role of mule driver. Does it ever happen to you? Here's a quick quiz to help you answer that question:

1. When it comes to a sport or other activity your teen's involved in, does your spouse or a friend ever tell you something like, "You need to back off a little, cut him some slack"?

2. If your teen asked you to back off, would your feelings be hurt?

3. Do you need to consciously calm yourself before attending your teen's performances?

4. Do you find yourself trying to play roles other than parent (coach, referee, judge, etc.) at your teen's events?

5. If your teen dropped a current activity, would it bother you more than it would her?

6. Has your teen, spouse, or other family member ever indicated embarrassment over your behavior at the teen's events?

7. If you did what you'd sometimes like to do to the coach, teacher, referee, or umpire, would you be arrested?

8. Have you ever said anything in anger or frustration at one of your teen's events that you later regretted?

9. Do you respond to your teen differently after an event, in terms of affection and encouragement, depending on whether he wins or loses?

10. Is your teen still pursuing any goal or activity, at your urging, that she has said at least twice she would like to drop?

Did you answer those questions as honestly as possible? If not, try again. If so, here's a simple guide to evaluating your responses:

- If you answered yes 8-10 times, see a counselor!
- If you answered yes 6-7 times, let a friend hold you accountable for improving.
- If you answered yes 4-5 times, give your teen permission to warn you when to back off.
- If you answered yes 1-3 times, reevaluate your attitudes and motives.

Another way to assess what kind of fragrance you're giving off is to ask your teen directly. Try these questions:

1. Do you feel more pressure when I'm watching you play or perform? If so, why?

2. If I said I'd like to sit down with you and talk about your performance in an event, would that make you feel good, or would it make you anxious? Why?

3. Do you feel as if any goals or activities have been forced on you? If so, which ones?

You don't need a guide to interpret your teen's answers to those questions. If they indicate a problem, make yourself accountable to your teen, your spouse, a friend, your pastor, or a counselor.

Your dream or your teen's? Which will it be?

You can choose today to be a mule driver or an encourager . . . an aroma of death, or the fragrance of life.

// WITH YOUR TEENAGER

Over homemade fruit smoothies at the kitchen table, try the following:

- Ask: "When it comes to a career, what do you think my dream is for you? How about when it comes to the kind of person you turn out to be?"
- Summarize the dreams you have for your teen. Reassure your teen, however, that your love for him or her doesn't depend on whether things turn out "your way."

• If, when you were a teen, you felt pressured by a person or circumstances to choose a particular activity or job, tell your teen what that was like. What did the experience teach you?

17

chill out!

*During the graduation ceremony, Bethany's parents
experienced a brief twinge of anxiety about her future.*

C lark had grown up in a strong Christian family. His dad was a preacher. His siblings took after their father. Clark, however, was the "different" child.

At age 17, he was into goofing off and playing pranks. School was drudgery to which he gave as little effort as possible. The future and his role in it were just a blur; he gave them no thought at all.

Naturally, Clark's parents felt deep concern. Their son had no direction, no goals. He had no passion for God, let alone any desire to use his gifts and talents in His service. What, they wondered as he approached high school graduation, would become of their unmotivated son?

There are a lot of teens like Clark.

It's not necessarily because they've been deprived or neglected. Many have been given everything they could want—toys, games, sports equipment. When they reach the teen years, they don't seem interested in career plans and independence. All they want to do is skateboard, talk on the phone with friends, and play Nintendo.

What can a parent with a teen like Clark do?

Remedial Training and Encouragement

If you find yourself with an unmotivated, directionless teen, some remedial training might be in order. If you've been in the habit of trying to provide anything he wants, tell him kindly but firmly the next time he makes a request, "From now on, you'll need to pay for half of things like that mountain bike yourself."

If he asks, "How am I supposed to do that?" answer, "Get a job. Earn some money."

Your teen may decide his wish list can be shorter. He may also begin to stretch and grow, applying some ingenuity, effort, and discipline toward getting what he wants. That may spur him to plan for longer-range goals as well.

» "My mom said constantly, 'Shoot for your dreams! Someday you are going to be something great! I love you.'"

—*Amanda*

When your teen makes any move in a positive direction—applying for an after-school job, sending for a college catalog, asking for your help in weighing career options—encourage her like crazy! Affirming, sincere words have amazing power:

- "Jenny, I'm proud of you for taking the initiative to get more information about those colleges you're interested in."
- "Sean, if those folks at the pet shop hire you, they're going to be getting the best young worker in town!"

- "Kimberly, I'm so glad you've applied to go on that missions trip! Who knows what you'll learn about God—and yourself—from that experience!"
- "John, you did a great job helping with the younger kids at VBS! Mrs. Smith couldn't say enough good things about you. Have you considered the possibility of becoming a teacher?"

Encouragement can take other forms as well:

- "Let's go get some ice cream together."
- "Let me help you fill out that form."
- "After you finish looking through that college catalog, what say we discuss it over a game of miniature golf?"

A little encouragement can get incredible results. As my friend and mentor Jack Herschend likes to say, it can even be used to teach a pigeon to bowl—in 20 minutes! How? You put the pigeon down near the bowling ball. Then, every time he takes a step toward the ball, you "encourage" him with a kernel of corn. Every time he touches the ball, you give him two. Soon he'll be pushing the ball down the alley.

Our teens, of course, are a lot smarter than pigeons. When we praise any accomplishment—even just a step on the road to accomplishment—we'll get more of the same behavior.

Are You Pushing?

Another way to deal with a seemingly unmotivated teen is to ask yourself if you're pushing too hard. I've seen many teens who felt their parents were "making too big a deal out of it" or were pressing in a direction the teens weren't sure about.

The teens' response was passive aggression. Unable to openly express their frustration, they resisted quietly by simply doing nothing. Here's what that can look like:

- Mom keeps telling Susie to send for college catalogs; that's the *last* thing Susie's about to do.

- Dad's constantly urging Jeff to get a part-time job; Jeff has no intention of asking anyone for—let alone filling out—an employment application.
- Mom thinks Dan was born to be a doctor, and she asks him at least once a week why he doesn't volunteer at the local hospital; Dan will keep finding excuses until the day she stops asking.
- Dad, who dreams of Shanna's becoming a classical concert pianist, has spent thousands of dollars on lessons she didn't really want; instead of working hard to get into a prestigious school like Juilliard, as he's always urging, she's practicing less and less each week.

If these examples of passive-aggressive behavior sound like what's going on at your house, consider whether you may be pushing too hard or in a direction your teen doesn't want to go. Ask your spouse for his or her assessment. Even better, ask your teen what he or she thinks—if you're sure you can handle the truth.

If you *are* pushing, pray for the humility—as so many of us parents have had to do so many times—to admit you were wrong and to start giving your teen some space.

There's Still Time

Your teen is a work in progress. He's learning, growing, developing. There's still time for him to consider options, try different things, talk to people, and find a direction. There's also time for the values you've modeled and the lessons you've taught to bear fruit.

When an unmotivated teen really wants something that you're not going to hand over on a silver platter, or the application deadline for the college of his choice is suddenly looming and he has yet to ask teachers to write letters of recommendation, motivation has a way of appearing in abundance.

If you've modeled a good work ethic, the joy of dreaming big for God, and the value of setting and pursuing goals consistent with those dreams, your teen probably will follow your example eventually. The driving forces will be your teen's felt need, the benefits to be gained (as demonstrated in your life), and the work of the Holy Spirit.

Clark, the young man introduced at the beginning of this chapter, *did* start thinking about his future as the end of his high school days came into view. He began to see his parents' devotion to God in a new light—as something that gave meaning to life and that he wanted to emulate. And a mentor, his youth pastor, gently encouraged him to get serious about his plans and consider attending a Christian college.

The Holy Spirit was at work in Clark's mind and heart as well. Did he really want to spend the rest of his life imagining the grades he *could* have earned, the skills he *could* have developed, the fulfilling life with God and service to Him that he *could* have enjoyed?

Clark picked a Christian college, and he went there determined to make the most of the opportunity. Forgoing some of the "fun" pursued by other students and enduring occasional hostility from less-motivated classmates, he earned straight A's and became a campus leader.

As Clark assessed how God had wired him, he concluded that his best career fit would be business and finance. He also saw it as a mission field. "If everyone were called to minister in the church," he said, "there would be no one to represent God in the secular arena."

Today, this former "slacker" is hard at work as a financial analyst for a bank in the Northeast. He's using his God-given interests and abilities every day, and he's doing his best to show God's love to friends, coworkers, and clients. If his parents could have seen all this when Clark was a teen, they might have breathed a very large sigh of relief.

The Never-Ending Story

Mom and Dad, remember Ephesians 2:10. It's as true for your teen as it is for any other Christian: "For we are God's workmanship, created in Christ Jesus to do good works, which God prepared in advance for us to do."

There's a reason God has wired your teen as He has. Whether it's through your child's career, church work, hobbies, or all of those and more, the Lord has plans to do great good through his or her life.

So chill out! The story of your child's growth into a mature, God-honoring young person is still being written.

There's still time. Neither you nor God is finished with your teen yet.

// WITH YOUR TEENAGER

Over a hot deep dish at your favorite pizza parlor, try the following:

- Ask: "Do you have a better idea of how to pursue God-honoring dreams than you did at the beginning of this process? What questions do you still have?"
- Ask: "What are a couple of key things you've learned about how God has wired you?"
- Ask: "What could be your next three steps in the pursuit of your dreams?"

notes

Chapter 3

1. Gary Smalley and John Trent, *The Two Sides of Love* (Colorado Springs, Colo.: Focus on the Family, 1990), p. 28.
2. James Dobson, *Complete Marriage and Family Home Reference Guide* (Wheaton, Ill.: Tyndale, 2000), pp. 302-3.
3. Smalley and Trent, *The Two Sides of Love*, pp. 32-36.
4. Ibid., pp. 37-99.

Chapter 4

1. Clyde Narramore, *How to Choose Your Life's Work* (Grand Rapids, Mich.: Zondervan, 1969), p. 29.
2. Richard Bolles, *What Color Is Your Parachute?* (Berkeley, Calif.; Ten Speed Press, 1978), pp. 93-94.
3. John William Zehring, *Get Your Career in Gear* (Wheaton, Ill.: Victor Books, 1976), pp. 75-76.

Chapter 8

1. Arlene Taylor, "Sensory Preference Assessment" (Napa, Calif.: Realizations, Inc., 2003). Copyright © 1984, 2003 by Arlene Taylor, Ph.D., with acknowledgment of work by Donald J. Moine, Ph.D. and input from I. Katherine Benziger, Ph.D. For more information see www.arlenetaylor.org.

Chapter 10

1. John C. Maxwell, *Breakthrough Parenting* (Colorado Springs, Colo.: Focus on the Family, 1996), p. 102.
2. Gary Smalley and Greg Smalley, *Bound by Honor* (Wheaton, Ill.: Tyndale/Focus on the Family, 1998), p. 167.
3. Ron Lee Davis, *Mentoring* (Nashville: Thomas Nelson, 1991), pp. 45-47.
4. Focus on the Family radio broadcast, "Encouraging Your Kids to Lead," October 3, 2002.

Chapter 11

1. Rick Warren, *The Purpose-Driven Life* (Grand Rapids, Mich.: Zondervan, 2002), p. 17.
2. Ibid., p. 69.
3. Ibid., p. 63.
4. Henry Blackaby and Claude King, *Experiencing God* (Nashville: Broadman & Holman, 1994), pp. 67-68, 55, 69.
5. Ibid., p. 157.
6. Ibid., pp. 125-26.
7. Ibid., pp. 69-71.
8. Erla Zwingle, "Megacities" (*National Geographic*, November 2002), pp. 77-78.
9. Philip Jenkins, *The Next Christendom* (New York: Oxford University Press, 2002), p. 9.
10. Warren, *The Purpose-Driven Life*, p. 39.

Chapter 12

1. George Barna, *Generation Next* (Ventura, Calif.: Regal, 1995), pp. 26-27.

Chapter 14

1. Michael Ryan, "An American Success Story" (*Parade*, June 30, 2002), pp. 4-5.
2. Ibid., p. 5.

FOCUS ON THE FAMILY.

Welcome to the *Family!*

Whether you received this book as a gift, borrowed it, or purchased it yourself, we're glad you read it. It's just one of the many helpful, insightful, and encouraging resources produced by Focus on the Family.

In fact, that's what Focus on the Family is all about—providing inspiration, information, and biblically based advice to people in all stages of life.

It began in 1977 with the vision of one man, Dr. James Dobson, a licensed psychologist and author of 18 best-selling books on marriage, parenting, and family. Alarmed by the societal, political, and economic pressures that were threatening the existence of the American family, Dr. Dobson founded Focus on the Family with one employee and a once-a-week radio broadcast aired on only 36 stations.

Now an international organization, the ministry is dedicated to preserving Judeo-Christian values and strengthening and encouraging families through the life-changing message of Jesus Christ. Focus ministries reach families worldwide through 10 separate radio broadcasts, two television news features, 13 publications, 18 Web sites, and a steady series of books and award-winning films and videos for people of all ages and interests.

• • •

For more information about the ministry, or if we can be of help to your family, simply write to Focus on the Family, Colorado Springs, CO 80995 or call (800) A-FAMILY (232-6459). Friends in Canada may write Focus on the Family, PO Box 9800, Stn Terminal, Vancouver, BC V6B 4G3 or call (800) 661-9800. Visit our Web site—www.family.org—to learn more about Focus on the Family or to find out if there is an associate office in your country.

We'd love to hear from you!

Resources to Help
Your Teen Grow

In a world where families are increasingly scattered and overscheduled, *Fuel* helps busy teens connect with their parents. Youth expert Joe White has put together powerful 10-minute devotions from the New Testament for you to share. It's fun, fast and filled with memorable stories, discussion starters and lifeline applications—all designed to get parents and teens talking. Paperback.
Fuel: 10-Minute Devotions to Ignite the Faith of Parents and Teens

Where do teen guys go when they have questions about their lives and the changes they're going through? All the issues facing today's guys are addressed and answered in this easy-to-read, engaging book. Honest and straightforward, *Boom* tackles physical changes, sexuality and dating, spiritual growth and more. An invaluable resource for parents who want to help their sons thrive during the teen years and explode into a man of God. Paperback.
Boom: A Guy's Guide to Growing Up

Teen girls have lots of questions about life. From changing bodies, to dating and sex, to relationships, money and more, girls will find the answers they need to understand this time in their lives and what it means to become a godly woman. Ideal for parents who want to help their daughters thrive during the teen years and bloom into womanhood. Paperback.
Bloom: A Girl's Guide to Growing Up

CROSSINGS®
THE BOOK CLUB FOR TODAY'S CHRISTIAN FAMILY

A Letter to Our Readers

Dear Reader:
In order that we might better contribute to your reading enjoyment, we would appreciate your taking a few minutes to respond to the following questions. When completed, please return to the following:

Andrea Doering, Editor-in-Chief
Crossings Book Club
401 Franklin Avenue, Garden City, NY 11530
You can post your review online! Go to www.crossings.com and rate this book.

Title _____ Author _____

1 Did you enjoy reading this book?

❑ Very much. I would like to see more books by this author!

❑ I really liked_____

❑ Moderately. I would have enjoyed it more if_____

2 What influenced your decision to purchase this book? Check all that apply.

   ❑ Cover
   ❑ Title
   ❑ Publicity
   ❑ Catalog description
   ❑ Friends
   ❑ Enjoyed other books by this author
   ❑ Other _____

3 Please check your age range:

   ❑ Under 18   ❑ 18-24
   ❑ 25-34   ❑ 35-45
   ❑ 46-55   ❑ Over 55

4 How many hours per week do you read? _____

5 How would you rate this book, on a scale from 1 (poor) to 5 (superior)?
   _____

Name_____

Occupation_____

Address_____

City_____ State_____ Zip_____